spectorgroup

ROCKPORT
PUBLISHERS

Rockport Publishers, Inc.
Rockport, Massachusetts

First published in the United States of America by:
Rockport Publishers, Inc.
146 Granite Street
Rockport, Massachusetts 01966
Telephone: (508) 546-9590
Fax: (508) 546-7141

Distributed to the book trade and art trade in the U.S. and Canada by:

The AIA Press
1735 New York Avenue
Washington, DC 20006
Telephone: 800-365-ARCH
Fax: 800-678-7102

Other Distribution by:
Rockport Publishers, Inc.
Rockport, Massachusetts 01966

ISBN 1-56496-117-6

10 9 8 7 6 5 4 3 2 1

Art Director: Laura Herrmann
Design Firm: Group C
Layout and Production: Kathleen Kelley
Cover Photograph: Andrew Kramer

Printed in China

Dedication
To my wife and best friend
Joan
whose faith in me was the spark for my self-confidence.

To my children
Scott, Marc, and Jolie
whose presence on this planet was my impetus to strive.

To my grandchildren
Alex Brooke, Charlie Harrison, and Jake Hunter
who are the twinkling stars of the future.

Acknowledgments   I've enjoyed being intricately involved in the process of creating this retrospective and could not have accomplished it without the many people who contributed to its fruition. I would like to thank Jane Felsen Gertler for her writing, leadership, and patience with my constant revisions, my son Marc Spector for a sensitive Afterword, my wife Joan for her fresh ideas and unique way with words, Kathleen Carey and Irene Lennon for their capable helping hands and the staff of the Spector Group who contributed their thoughts and energy in capturing nearly thirty years of architecture.

It is important to thank the many people who were collaborators. My partners, Dominic Cardone, Peter K. Toh, and Michael J. Mannetta, are as focused as I am in attempting to ensure the highest level of quality in every project we do. My gratitude to them is immeasurable. The list of collaborators shows how many people have dedicated themselves to our firm and our profession.

— Michael Harris Spector

Table of Contents

6 Preface

Buildings and Projects

8 Allstate Insurance Company

12 Great Neck Estates Apartments

14 Extebank

18 IBM • Jericho Plaza

22 Dime Savings Bank Headquarters

24 666 Old Country Road

26 Avant Garde Optics

28 European American Bank Plaza

34 IBM Research Group

38 New York Hilton Hotel

40 Spector Group Studios

46 United States Postal Service

48 Chase Manhattan Bank, Garden City

52 NYNEX Headquarters

56 Merrill Lynch Computer Center

62 Merck & Company

66 Merrill Lynch Executive Group

70 40 and 80 Cuttermill Road

74 Grumman Data Systems

82 Long Island Savings Bank

90 Metropolis

92 Ivy Tower

94 Roslyn Highlands Firehouse

98 Long Island University

104 Ronald McDonald House

106 Maimonides Medical Center

108 Horizon One

112 Fleet Bank Corporate Headquarters

116 Key Bank Headquarters

120 General Accident Insurance Company

124 Country Glen Center

126 River Run Community

128 Century Condominiums

132 Hewlett-Woodmere School District

136 Woodbury Jewish Center

138 Computer Associates International World Headquarters

146 Temple Judea Holocaust Resource Center

148 Chase Manhattan Bank Plaza, New York

150 BMW Showroom and Service Pavilion

154 Sony Western Regional Operations Center

158 Cablevision Corporate Headquarters

160 Nove Butovice Technology City, Prague

162 People's Republic of China

    Zhong Hang Plaza

    San Kei Commercial City

    Fashion City Central

    Jiu Hai Plaza

168 Federal Building and United States Courthouse

170 Meadowlands Town Center

173 Afterword

174 Representative Project Portfolio

188 Awards

190 Collaborators

191 Photographers

Charles Sanford Spector, 1935

Preface

A sensitive, delicate watercolor of the Parthenon painted by my father sixty years ago graces the wall of my office as I write. I muse at the thought of how far I've traveled since I first saw that picture during my childhood, and how becoming an architect like him was subtly implanted in my mind way back then. How amazed and thrilled he would be if he were here to witness the course of events that have catapulted me and now my two sons, Scott and Marc, into the continuing and demanding challenge of creating good architecture.

I learned quickly when I started my own firm, Michael Harris Spector, A.I.A. in 1965, that to become successful one had to go beyond being a good designer, that consideration and awareness of my client's needs and feelings was a priority and demanded recognition. I realize now that this was my first step in acknowledging that architecture was indeed a partnership, whether it be with clients, contractors, consultants, or staff members. My ability to communicate understanding, foster confidence, and earn trust so I could educate was a tremendous necessity. When communication is optimal and enthusiasm is generated the design process flows. A palpable rhythm occurs.

The firm grew. More and more people joined me. We moved into our own building and became known as the Spector Group. Architecture now was the business of architecture and I was challenged with how to keep in touch with a larger staff, manage bigger projects, and indeed, perpetuate that personal interaction that had been one of the hallmarks of my success.

I recognized too that it was crucial for staff members of Spector Group to learn good communication skills among themselves as well as with individuals they worked with outside the office. We started a bimonthly group meeting facilitated by my wife, Dr. Joan Spector, who works as a clinical social worker. The purpose of this group was to create a safe environment for people to discuss feelings, concerns, thoughts, and ideas related to their workplace. No seniority existed in this meeting. As trust built, juniors and managers conversed openly and were free to agree and disagree with each other. An example was set; staff were allowed input and opinions and management would not be threatened. The partnership within our walls began to take shape.

This group became a forum during the eighties and into the nineties. The atmosphere of openness spread to our monthly office meetings and other office conferences.

Our keen awareness of the importance of partnering leads us to new challenges as we move into the twenty-first century and are faced with dealing in the international community. Would the Spector Group's interactional philosophy carry over to the foreign marketplace?

Prague, Brussels, and Shanghai appear to be responding positively. In Shanghai, because of the incredible cultural differences, I was particularly delighted to discover how receptive the Chinese were to my outreach of friendship and intellectual sharing of western architectural philosophy and technology. This advanced further when six Chinese architects spent three months working side by side with the Spector Group staff here in the United States on a joint project for Shanghai. They spoke no English, but communication and camaraderie flourished. It was the birth of a new partnership.

I stood among the columns of the Parthenon in Athens twenty years ago. I was awed by history that I could touch with my fingers, by the span of time that had elapsed since its inception. I am struck that I too am a creator of architecture, but do not stand alone. All those I work with have helped produce everything you will see on these pages. They are my real partners.

– Michael Harris Spector, FAIA

Allstate Insurance Company Farmingville, New York

The Allstate Insurance Company Headquarters, set in rural Suffolk County, New York, was one of the first major buildings constructed in this former farmland community. Located on forty-four acres of rolling terrain, this white, precast concrete structure is set on the knoll of Bald Hill, the highest point on Long Island. Grass berms accentuate the rolling terrain while giving human scale to this horizontal 258,000-square-foot structure.

Taking advantage of the natural contours of the site, this facility steps from two to three levels. Three floors of administrative functions surround a two-story lobby and reception area. This public space links the work areas with a large cafeteria capable of seating 850 employees. The majority of the structure is post and beam construction, with 125-foot clear spans of post-tensioned concrete, used in this region for the first time.

To limit sun infiltration, twelve-foot overhangs shade the perimeter. Each floor structure is expressed, allowing patterns of shadows to play against the facades. Parking for 3,000 vehicles is in three main areas, separated from each other by green belts and berms.

In 1970, when Ross Workman, Vice-President, stated, "You're a very young firm," I responded, "Give me a chance." He had trust and faith knowing it was our first major corporate headquarters. – Michael Harris Spector

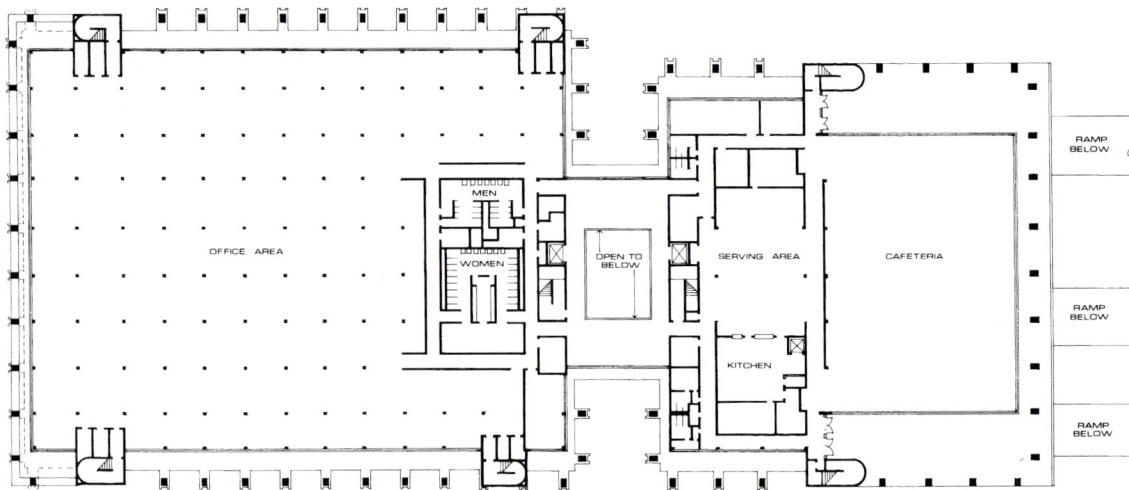

SECOND FLOOR PLAN

Allstate's Corporate Headquarters reflects its lofty hilltop location with soaring 125-foot clear spans and dramatic twelve-foot overhangs.

Great Neck Estates Apartments   Great Neck, New York

Set in a historic district of the Great Neck, New York peninsula, this apartment complex pays homage to the adjacent residential environment. The original buildings which are ripe with ornamental detail date back to the 1930s.

The parti of this new, 450-unit residential building design is a breakdown of massing to relate to different fabric on each perimeter orientation. The inner courtyard is reminiscent of old cloisters and gardens, providing views, water, and an area of greenery and relaxation for residents. Window and balcony treatments respond to exterior configurations of the historical surroundings and formulate their own referentiality.

Common facilities, including a small theatre, fitness center, restaurant, and meeting rooms, are located on the plaza level of the complex.

Extebank Hauppauge, New York

Alluding to the Villa Savoye, one of Le Corbusier's finest works, Extebank's new headquarters' building is an extreme architectural departure for the rural Suffolk County landscape.

Its purity and simplicity of form is mechanistic in feeling, fitting directly into its site—the V-shaped intersection of two major highways. The stark white porcelain metal panels are a positive contrast to the surroundings of dark greenery and paving. It projects its surroundings to passers-by through reflective glass windows which are gasketed into, and flush with, the panels.

Extebank's sculptural quality is achieved by its verticality in predominantly flat surroundings and by an arrangement of elements that are composed for equal interest from any view. The banking floor is freely defined by a number of enclosed forms containing specific functions such as the vault and stairs. It is capped by a rectangular floor of flexibly planned offices. Drive-in teller windows are located within the building.

A gem in Suffolk County . . .
"Le Corbusier's influence on Spector's
work is quite apparent and executed
beautifully." – Jury, AIA

In the 1920s Le Corbusier exemplified the essence of a revolutionary architect. His timeless design, inspirational to this day, gives us the impetus to dare to be bold and innovative. Extebank is one of the earliest examples of modern architecture in this rural area.

GROUND LEVEL

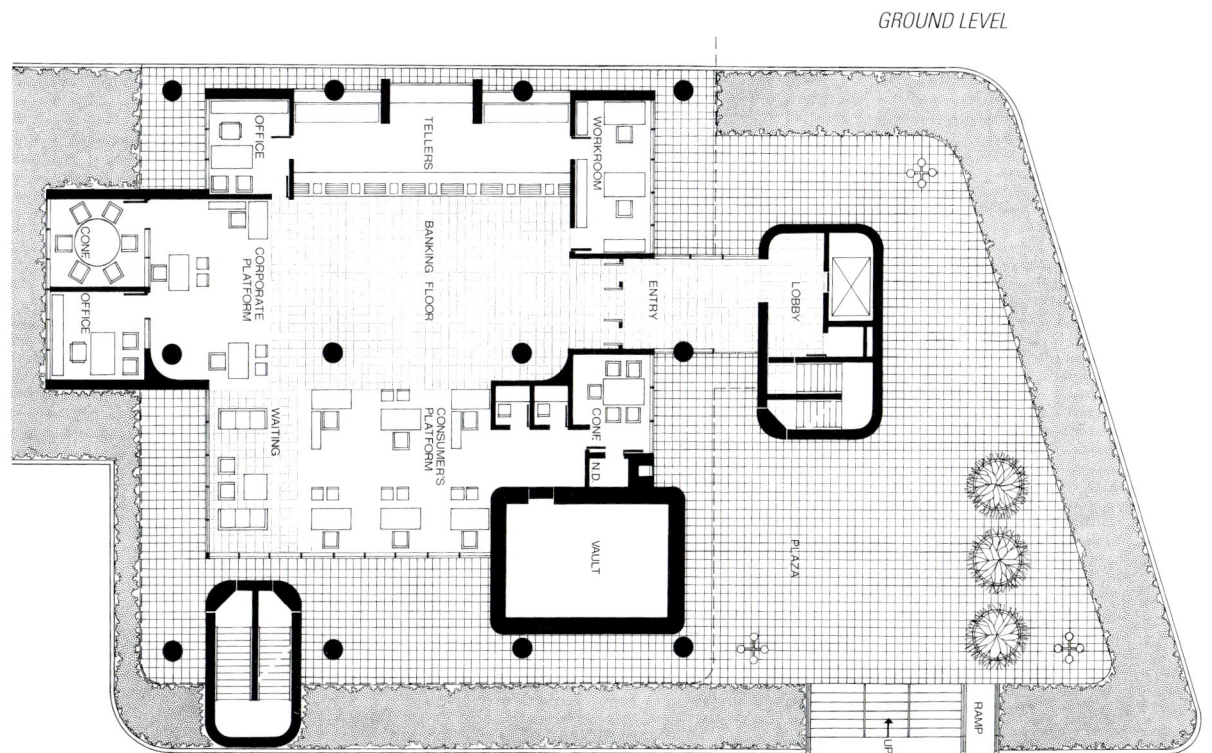

OFFICE
TELLERS
WORKROOM
CONF.
OFFICE
CORPORATE PLATFORM
BANKING FLOOR
ENTRY
LOBBY
WAITING
CONSUMER'S PLATFORM
CONF.
N.D.
VAULT
PLAZA
UP
RAMP

17

IBM • Jericho Plaza Jericho, New York

Simple geometry was altered slightly in this mid-1970s building, creating an architectural solution that is still controversial today. Surrounded by a green belt and fronting on the region's most highly traveled freeway, IBM presents a dynamic silhouette to the speeding passersby.

Upon entry, angular walls within a space-framed atrium define the central lobby area. The angles serve as a guide, leading the visitor to their respective vertical cores—two three-story parallel structures. The wings are juxtaposed with a two-bay offset, giving the illusion of impending motion. The floor area increases proportionately with height, in accordance with IBM blocking requirements. In addition, ground coverage was restrictive on grade.

An early use of glass and neoprene gasketing allows clean uninterrupted fenestration to alternate with the precast concrete facade. Coupled with the space-framed atrium, this building represents the beginning of an era of new concepts, where design, innovative systems, and materials combine, allowing contemporary architecture to break away from basic forms.

UPPER LEVEL

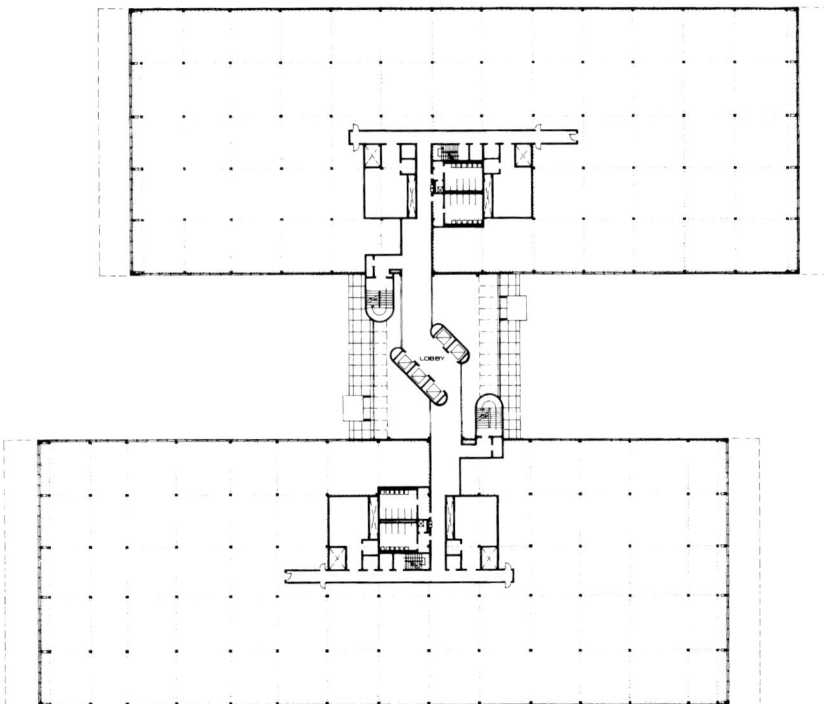

19

A series of geometric illusions challenge the mind. Coupled with angular facades and the appearance of motion, the architecture of Jericho Plaza stimulates interest in the company, and the people who work there.

After twenty-two years, the "Boat Buildings"
are still generating commentary as drivers
cruise down the Expressway.

Dime Savings Bank Headquarters Port Washington, New York

Within the suburban environment of Main Street, Port Washington, a historic peninsula on Long Island's North Shore, two adjacent buildings were connected and retrofitted to create a branch bank and regional offices for the Dime Savings Bank. With an architectural program that continually expanded, this structure introduced the form, color, and texture of contemporary architecture to the community.

A sculpted white, precast facade presents a bold appearance on this avenue of low-rise, turn-of-the-century buildings. A composition of deep recesses creates shadows that contrast with its strong profile. Large and small glass areas punctuated with open terraces are set back to reflect strength and security. A stair tower and column, expressed on the exterior, add further dimension to this bold architectural statement.

Warm wood and color define the interior banking and retail space in contrast with white columns and black ceramic pavers. Curved seating elements parallel polished oak work surfaces.

Shadows and recesses add
drama to the streetscape—
generating interest and providing relief from the sun.

BELLEVIEW AVENUE ELEVATION

REAR ELEVATION

666 Old Country Road   Garden City, New York

Adjacent to one of the largest retail malls in the northeastern United States, 666 Old Country Road stands majestically above the commercial clatter of the region. It is a site where three major highways converge and therefore is attractive to businesses seeking urban quality amenities in a growing suburban landscape.

In its sculptural form and relationship to human scale, 666 Old Country Road is heavily influenced by the theories of Mies van der Rohe and Le Corbusier. In the continuing Spector evolution of the pure glass box, these 1,600 panes of silver-mirrored glass are resolved to reflect not only the changing skies, but also the structure itself. Images are manipulated as the glass curtain wall evolves to its next phase. Deep, horizontal recesses punctuate the facade, defining the floors and adding negative space to this simple form. Rounded corners soften the building envelope. The stainless steel entry and lobby is set back one half column bay.

One is captured by its mercurial image. The building rises above its surroundings, reflecting only structure and sky.

Avant Garde Optics   Port Washington, New York

Begun in 1978, the headquarters of Avant Garde Optics is a dynamic blend of nature and the future. Distinguished in the world of imported eyewear, the partners of Avant Garde welcome clientele to their offices and showrooms to select from their European-based product line. By designing their warehouse and distribution center as one facility composed of two distinct components, the Spector Group and Avant Garde make a statement to their clients that reflects grandeur and discipline.

The architectural solution coupled a rolling natural landscape with the most modern design and the latest construction materials. Peering over a slight knoll, the blue and white office and distribution center appears as a one-story structure, giving no hint of its 185,000-square-foot interior, sixty percent of which is underground. The white office structure is distinct yet united with the blue warehouse which is configured as an exploded barn and silo. A wall of vision glass follows the perimeter of the office space. Offices share vistas of the nearby harbor and glass balconies overlook the natural environment.

Color and sculptural geometric proportions were influenced by the company's high-profile business and native European background. In addition, this building is an example of one of the earliest uses of aluminum-paneled exteriors in the country.

European American Bank Plaza Uniondale, New York

Set on thirty-six landscaped acres in Long Island, New York at the crossroads of two major highways, this gleaming 1.1 million-square-foot complex is the largest commercial office building in the region. With two elliptical towers of green reflective glass and matching monolithic spandrels, the poured-in-place, post-tensioned concrete structure allows for long spans between core and perimeter and for a virtually column-free, 30,000-square-foot floor design. The 46-foot dimension from core to window is a developed standard now employed by the real estate industry. The innovative use of flying forms made possible the simultaneous construction of the two towers and their topping out in less than eleven months.

State-of-the-art energy and space management systems set an unequaled standard for the office environment. Tenant efficiency, flexibility, and comfort is achieved through fully modular interior systems, computerized building operations, and column-free floor design with abundant window space for visual participation with the exterior.

To provide a sense of community for over 4,000 employees and visitors, public amenities became a major part of the design concept. A 55-foot-high, glass-domed winter garden surrounds a tropical setting of lush foliage, where a pedestrian walkway guides the public toward the sights and sounds of a two-story waterfall.

An exterior water sculpture converts to an ice rink for recreation in the winter months. The plaza truly becomes a gathering place as it ties together amenities and circulation functions, lending a cosmopolitan atmosphere to this suburban setting.

CUTAWAY AXONOMETRIC

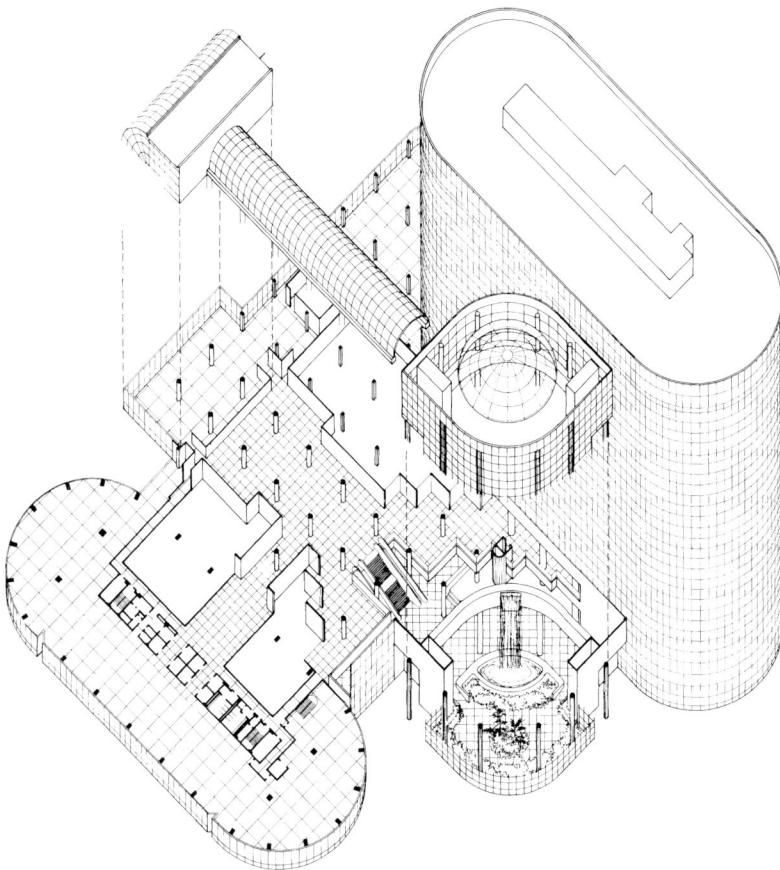

At the first annual Christmas tree lighting ceremony, the plaza came alive with people singing carols, children ice skating, and everyone sharing this exciting space. A dream for Long Island was realized.

EAB Plaza's two fifteen-story elliptical towers rise above a three-story podium. The landscaped thirty-six-acre building site was once an Air Force base.

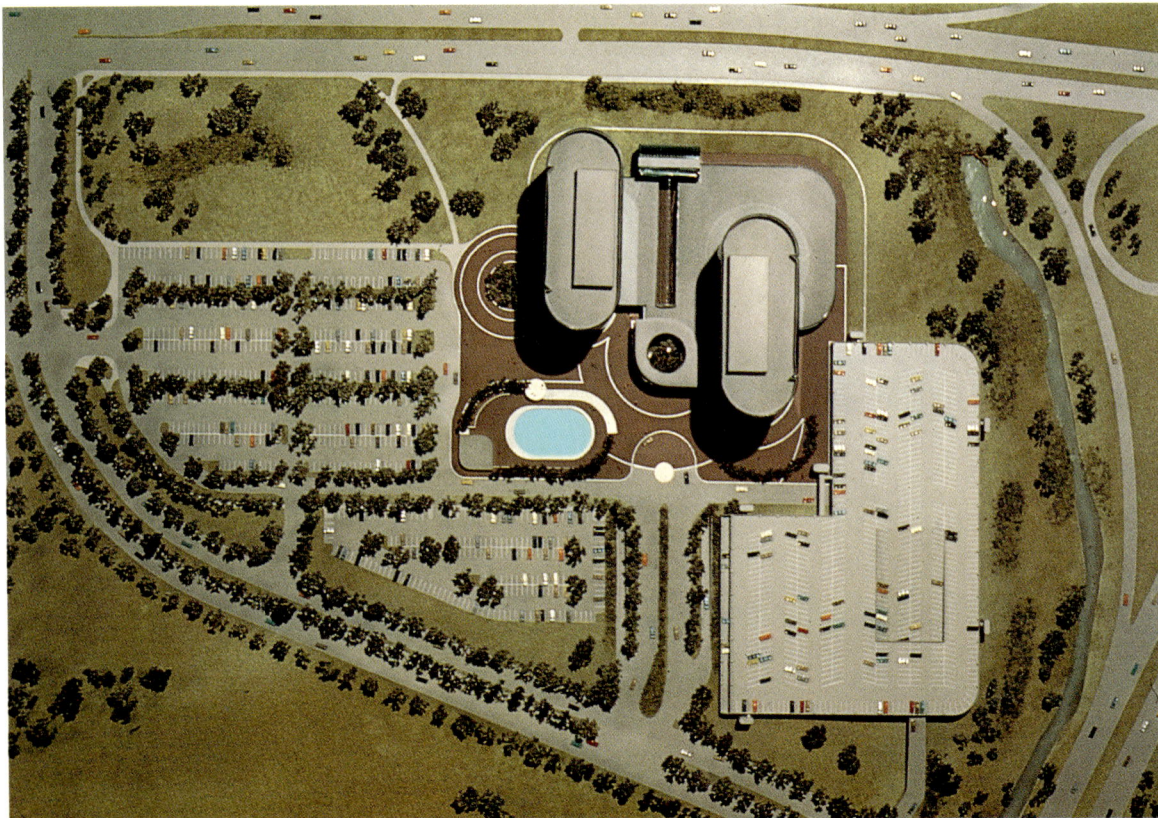

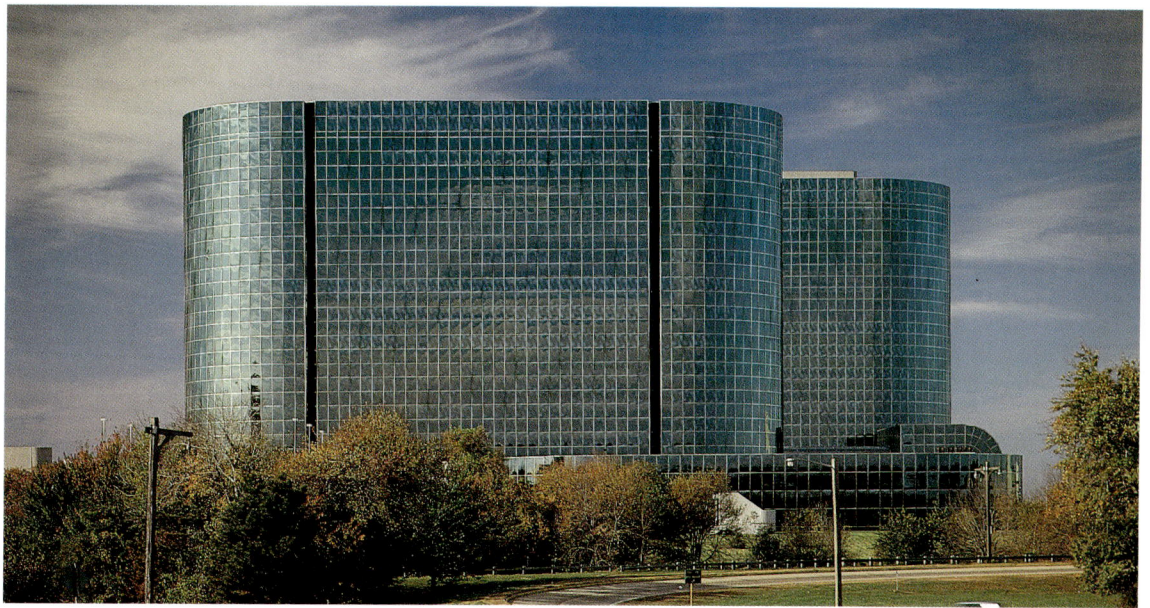

EAB had a vision: To create a unique environment in a rapidly growing region. They termed it the "Rockefeller Center of Long Island," a single expanse where people could work, dine, shop, or enjoy the amenities. Public space was pivotal to the concept.

IBM Research Group   Mt. Pleasant, New York

Reflecting the surrounding environment of rock, forest, and sky, IBM's silver glass research facility is a showcase for nature and business. It is dramatically juxtaposed with angled facades and a linear recessed notch. Its carved form carries the glass building further in its evolution, appearing as an extrusion of architecture. The sharp, irregular shape manipulates the material and references the inner workings of IBM's high-technology components.

Structural steel was the key to achieving a vital geometric format for this building while staying within specified cost parameters. Steel sections, cantilevered great distances away from the main frame of the building, create the unsupported sculptural proportions of the balconies. A sixty-foot span and suspended glass entry wall allows uninterrupted vision into a major atrium space where polished aluminum ceilings reflect black granite and ceramic floors.

Lighting, hidden in coves above and surrounding the elevator cores, interplays with adjacent surfaces to enhance the drama of the entry. Accenting the reception area of this 240,000-square-foot center is a three-story structural form which offers the illusion of unbraced descension.

The single exposed column is the focal point from which everything radiates. Behind it, a suspended glass wall virtually disappears, uniting the exterior plaza and the atrium. A series of columns, from front to rear, create a directional reference.
– Michael J. Mannetta

New York Hilton Hotel New York, New York

The two-phase renovation of this renowned hotel required an in-depth analysis of traffic and pedestrian movement. Towering above Manhattan's Rockefeller Center, this hotel giant demanded a design solution that focused on functionality, efficiency, vehicular and pedestrian accessibility, and image.

With much of the lobby movement derived from the hotel's premier banquet facilities and ballrooms, it was imperative to architecturally establish an open atmosphere of grace, beauty, and elegance. By combining all entrances, a unified space was created whereby the porte cochere is part of the hotel and not an extension of the avenue. Materials were chosen for exterior dexterity and their continued articulation throughout the lobby interior.

A curvilinear, polished stainless steel clad vestibule and fountain create the visual focus of the hotel. Ambiance is expounded by linear cold-cathode lighting while the granite driveway, rhythmically patterned in size, area, and color, creates an intimate scale.

Phase II of the hotel renovation includes plans for resurfacing the existing four-story building podium which houses ballroom facilities in granite. The design of horizontal banding in appropriate scale harmonizes with the surrounding towers to further the porte cochere statement. Continual recessed lighting will be installed to create a ceremonial yet romantic presence for this flagship hotel.

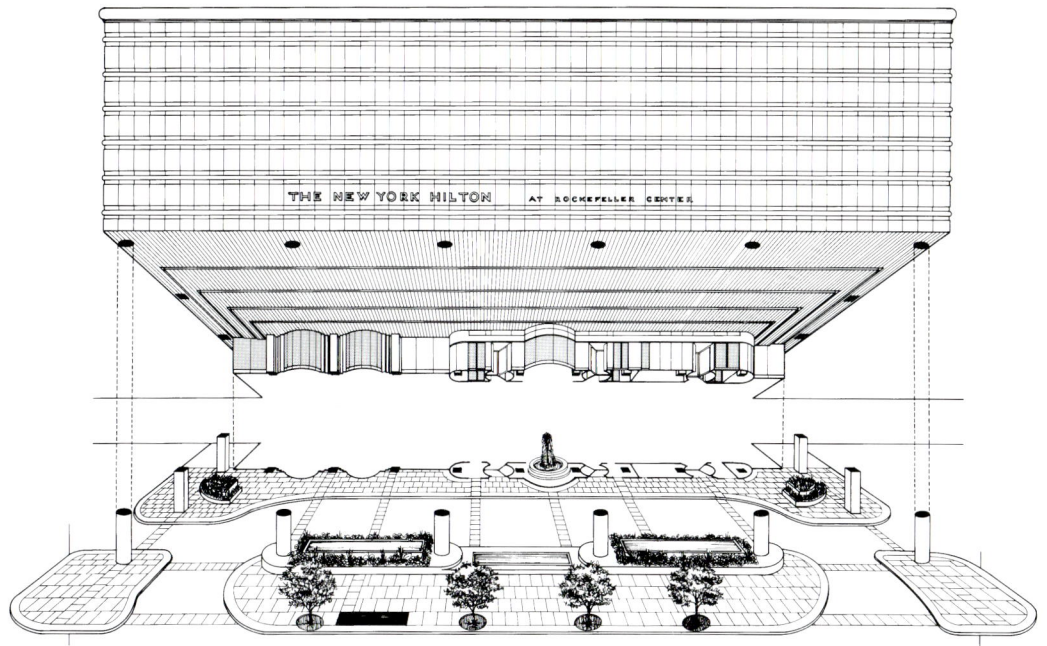

The hotel's original entrance disappeared within its framework. In the tumultuous environment of midtown Manhattan, the redesigned entrance is a distinctive and inviting porte cochere that exploits the exciting interaction of light and polished steel.

39

Spector Group Studios   North Hills, New York

The Spector Group chose an irregularly shaped, two-acre site nestled between two major parkways for the site of its new studios. A program was developed that called for a 20,000-square-foot structure. The architectural solution was a two-story facility that took advantage of the site's sloping terrain and permitted private grade-level entries to each of the two floors.

Out of respect for a residential development directly across the thoroughfare, a greige wire-cut brick and solar gray-tinted glass were chosen as the major exterior materials. Brightly painted handrails and columns provide a counterpoint to the brick and glass and create accents at the building entries and cantilevered terraces. The forms, articulation of its massing, and fenestration present a dignified profile and create a sense of harmony with the site.

Finished ceilings were eliminated from all spaces, except the internal core, to achieve greater height. Open web joists, HVAC ducts, lighting, and hung planters give the ceiling a woven pattern of lace, mass, and color while exposing the elements of architecture to clients and staff.

Contact with the exterior is enhanced by the placement of glass, with sunlight controlled by deep overhangs on the east and west orientations. Both natural and indirect lighting are used to create a bright, energetic environment.

Light, structure, space, and, above all, energy.
For our clients and ourselves.

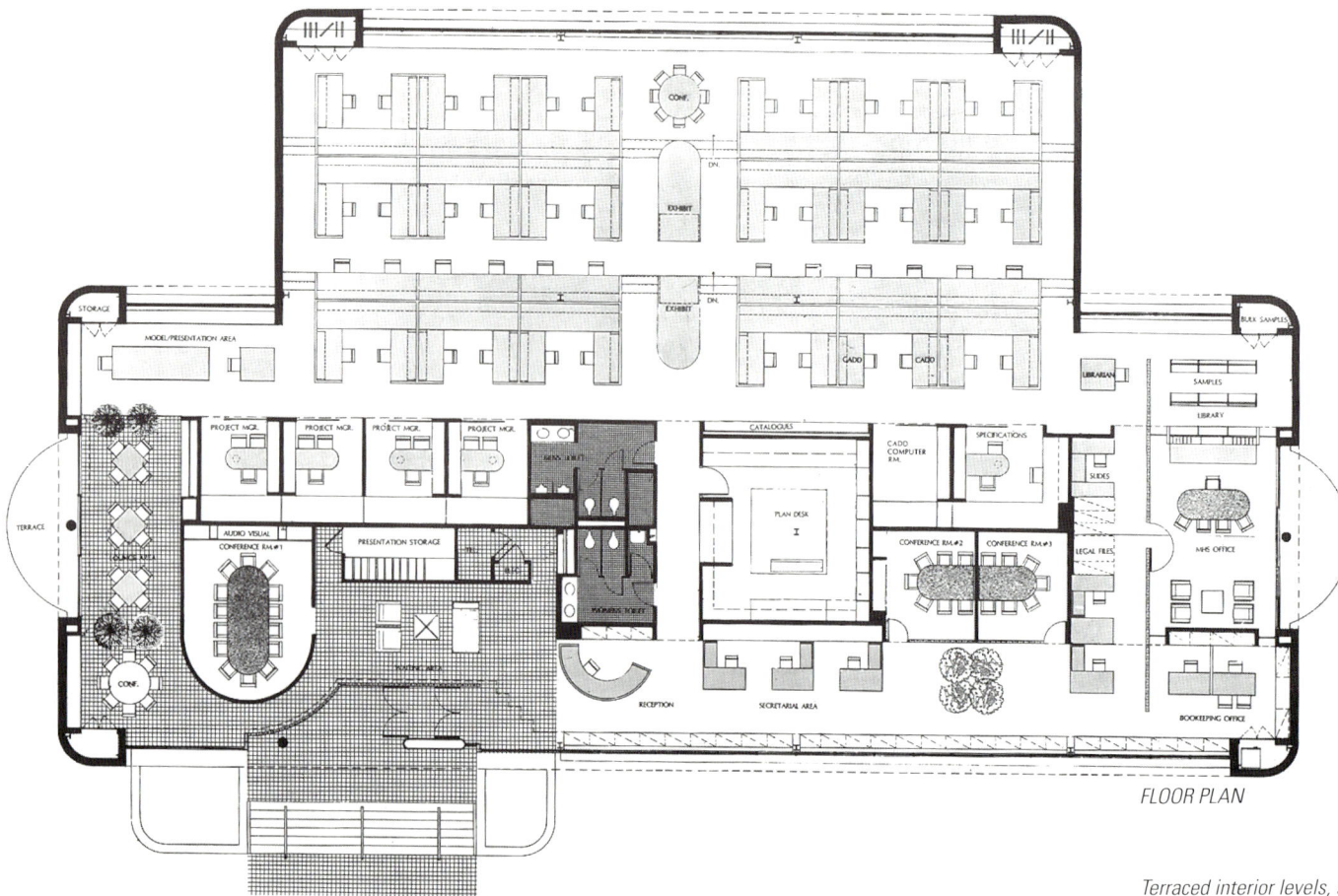

FLOOR PLAN

Terraced interior levels, set amidst greenery, project
clusters of open workstations with woodland views.
Communication and the exchange of ideas becomes
easy as visual contact is enhanced. Definitions of space
exist, yet the height of the workspace allows freedom
of thought and imagination.

United States Postal Service Hicksville, New York

The United States Postal Service Mid-Island Mail Processing Facility is one of the world's most modern automated "mail factories." It processes hundreds of thousands of letters per hour for three million businesses and residents. The building is also the national prototype for the Postal Service's "Total Energy" concept.

Designed in a joint venture with the Hillier Group, the 258,000-square-foot processing center saves an astounding 74 percent, or $900,000 per year on its utility bill, compared with similar, conventional buildings. These savings result from an innovative use of underground aquifers and additional energy-saving technology.

In this closed system, cool water is drawn from the aquifer during summer months to help cool the large, single-story buildings. As the water dissipates its coolness, it is returned at a higher temperature to the aquifer, where it is stored in a natural "bulb." During the heating season, the relatively hot water is brought back and used to help heat the building.

Other energy-saving advances include the use of propane, a clean fuel for heating, and the use of 386 skylights combined with photosensor, or "only when needed" artificial lighting. In addition, the building structure consists of insulated, precast concrete.

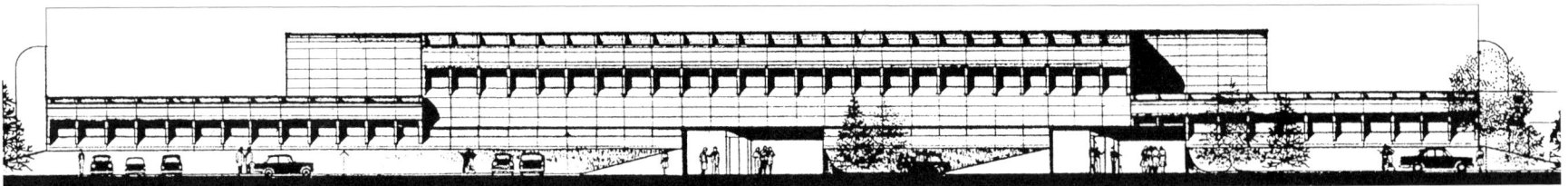

FRONT ELEVATION

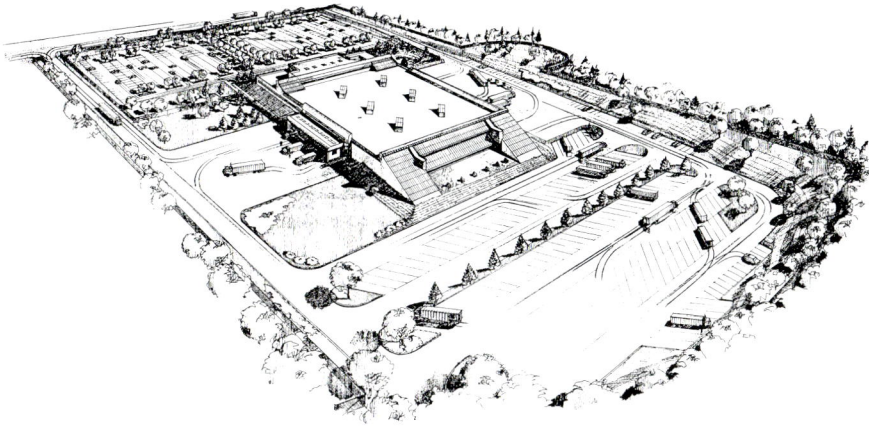

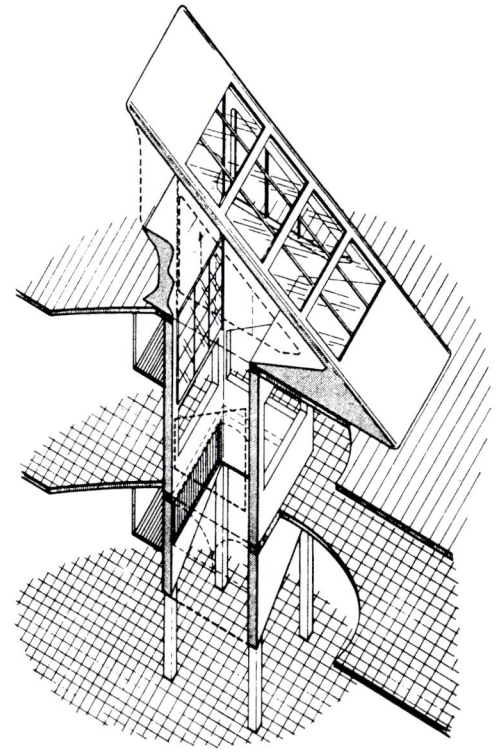

FRESH AIR INTAKE

Chase Manhattan Bank   Garden City, New York

Mitchel Field, often referred to as midtown Long Island, is home to regional offices for Chase Manhattan Bank. Two identical six-story buildings are linked by plazas and walkways to form a 420,000-square-foot corporate center.

Dominating the north side of the western building is a 180-foot-long by 50-foot-high atrium. A curving glass facade allows natural light in by day and, when illuminated in the evening, is a strong yet complementary form amidst the building's glass and aluminum exterior. The eastern building is identical in design. Both facilities were sited to reveal two important elevations to the main avenue—the atrium of one and the stepped corner of the other. Two paved plazas become one as they interweave their patterns and unite the buildings at ground level.

Eight hundred underground parking spaces are connected to the building by elevators. Landscaped lightwells, located on the building perimeters, allow daylight into below-grade parking areas. An additional seven hundred spaces are located on grade. Surrounding the complex is a landscaped plaza with sitting areas and walkways, which further unite this corporate complex.

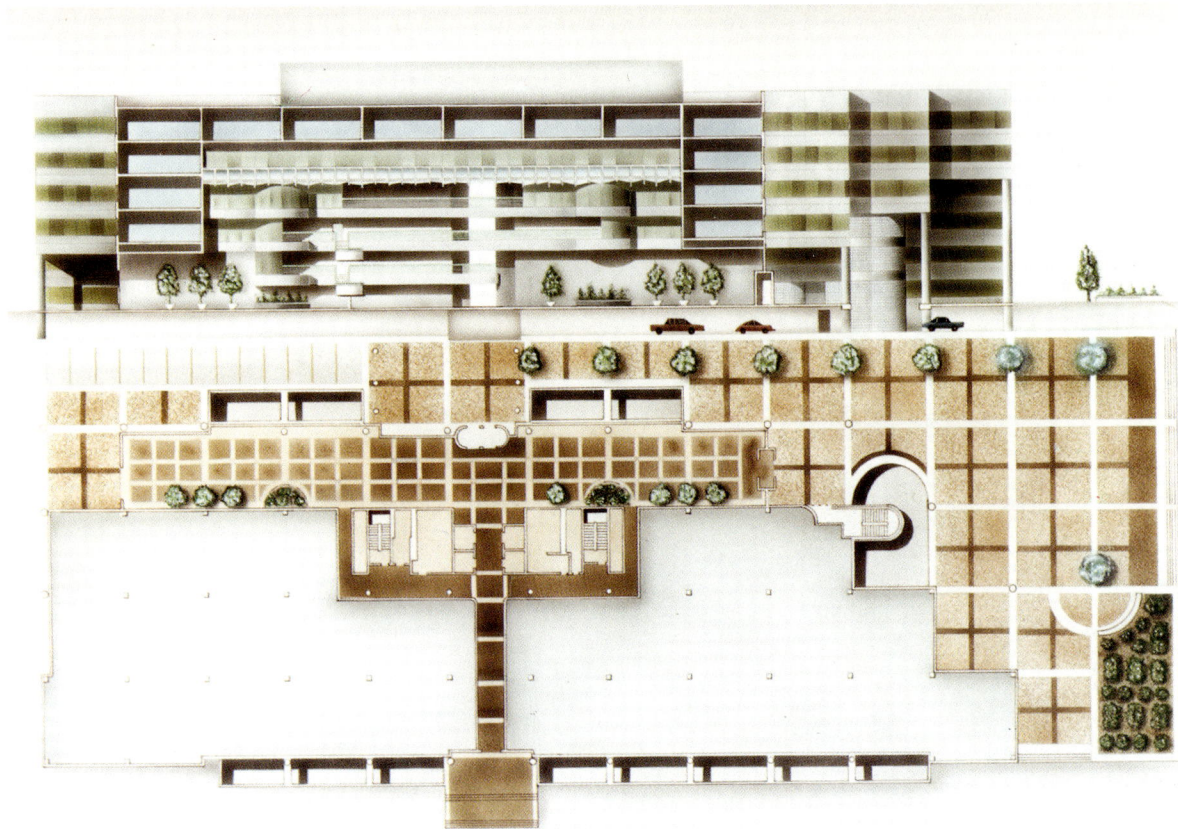

ENTRY DETAIL

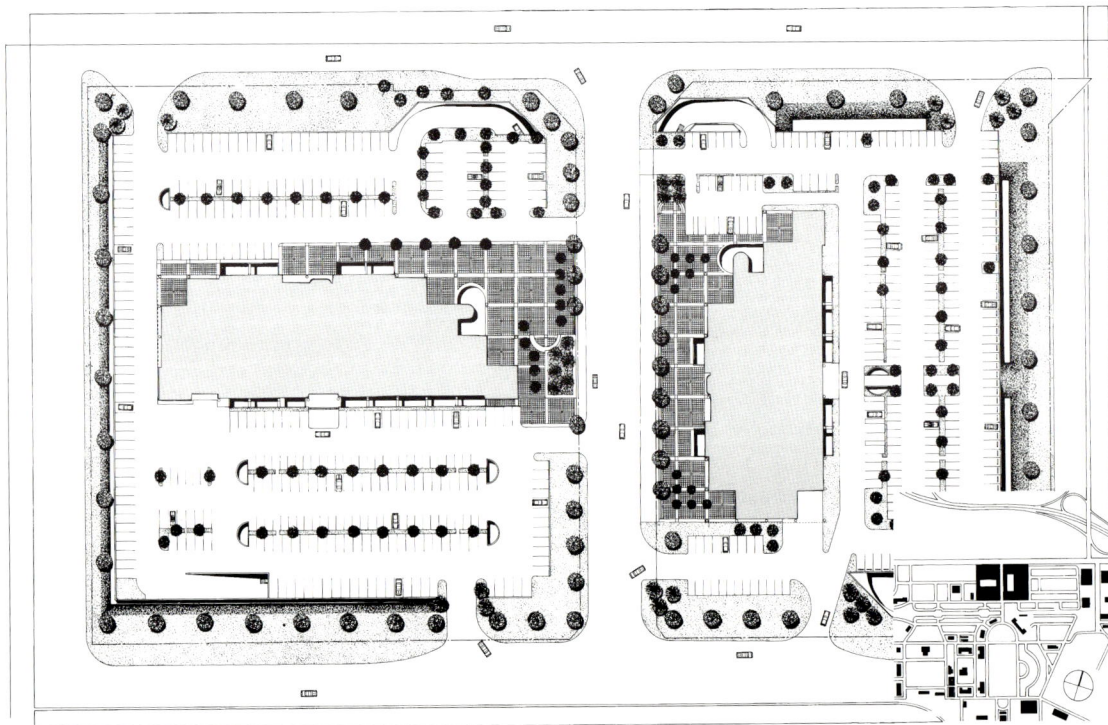

SITE PLAN

Cantilevered office and reception areas rise to the full height of the building and overlook the glass atrium below.

NYNEX Headquarters   White Plains, New York

Located on twenty-five acres of dramatically rolling, rock-studded terrain, NYNEX's corporate headquarters was designed to accentuate the natural sloping contours of the site. The two-building configuration cascades down the hillside and becomes an extension of the natural terrain. This 425,000-square-foot complex achieves site integration by using pedestrian plazas to serve as a connection between two business groups. The plaza's natural rock aggregate blends with the environment, in contrast to the building's sleek horizontal facade.

Alternating ribbons of glass and stone disappear and return as the facades complete their curvilinear forms. The pedestrian paths follow these contours as well, moving within the site. The articulate manipulation of light-colored, custom-designed precast concrete panels, paired with green energy-efficient reflective glass affords a sleek, textural quality. This detail is further established by the carving of reveals. Flanked by a three-story colonnade and suspended glass wall, the elliptical curved entryways are the visual focal point of each building. Dramatic atrium lobbies, capped with skylit spaceframes, appear to float within the confines of the colonnade.

To build a headquarters on the side of a mountain is a monumental task. J. Michael Divney, our site engineer, is a genius, and a man I consider a very close friend. – Michael Harris Spector

EXECUTIVE WING – GROUND FLOOR PLAN

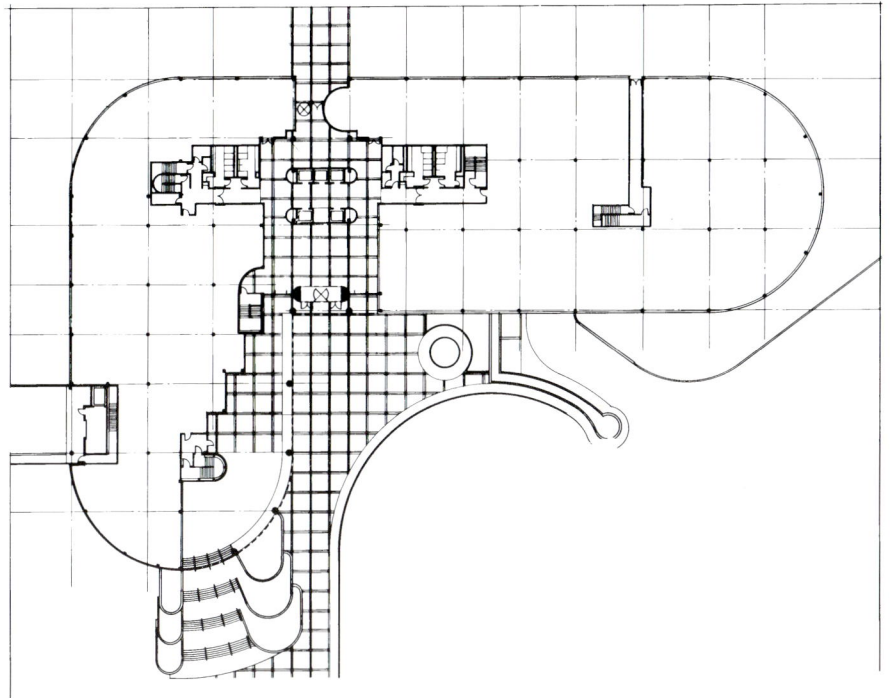

Merrill Lynch Computer Center   Somerset, New Jersey

This financial giant required a building located on a central New Jersey site to house its computer groups. The architectural program called for a dynamic image and an innovative design solution sensitive to the surrounding corporate environs. Budget was the main challenge in solving the program.

Time-tested materials were combined with state-of-the-art technology to create a lifespace that enhances productivity and corporate image and even goes further to promote a feeling of well being and a sense of alliance with elements of the earth.

The building plan optimizes the floor area, permitting great flexibility for support services. Views and vistas, both interior and exterior, are plentiful as the concept of bringing the exterior environment within succeeds. The vitality of the entrance atrium/solarium creates an area of dominance and symbolism.

In the atrium, all elements come to life as a four-story geyser creates an exhilarating expression of power harnessed within. It carves a space vertically, producing a four-story light well, capped by a skylit dome. Perimeter balconies overlook the entire atrium area and beckon all to participate in this space.

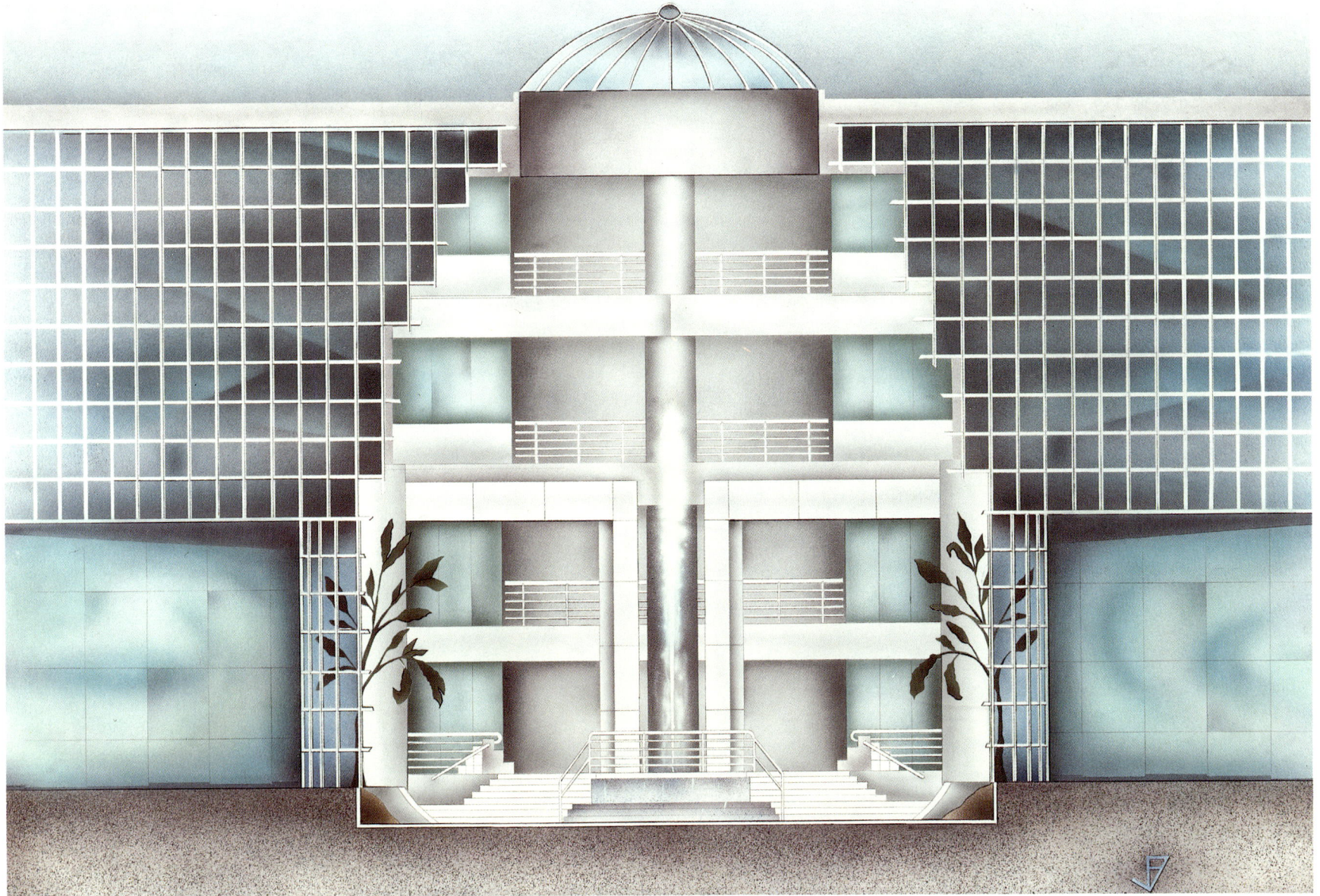

DETAIL SECTION

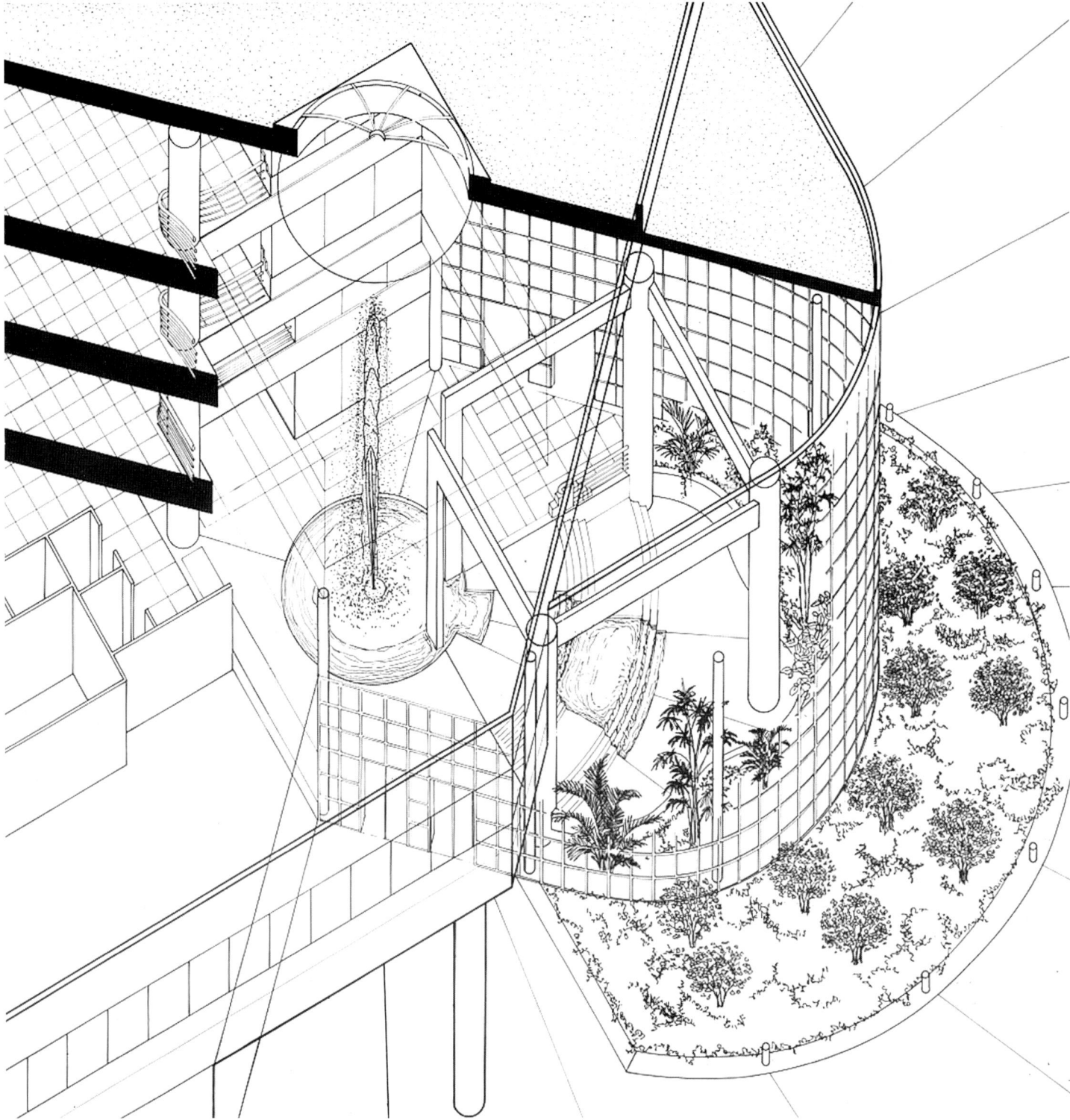

CUTAWAY AXONOMETRIC THROUGH ATRIUM

Merck & Company Somerset, New Jersey

Strategically positioned within a 94-acre corporate park, Merck & Company's regional headquarters is sited at the highest elevation of Somerset County. As the final project within this corporate campus, the headquarters completes and unifies the complex. This 200,000-square-foot building incorporates the same materials and elements used in the design of the four adjacent facilities.

The exterior wall of green granite tile and ribbon windows creates an envelope sympathetic to its neighboring facades. A colonnade punctuates the front facade and defines a pedestrian arcade to the main entrance of the building. The entry area is enhanced by a vertical stairwell encased in a tower of glass block.

Exposed flying bridges link interior spaces and maintain a sense of openness within the five-story skylit atrium. The suspended glass facade is enhanced by the inclusion of green plantings and a series of mobile sculptures. The public space within the plaza area contains serpentine seating and dining areas for conversation and relaxation.

Illuminated from within, the tower glows like a beacon in the night and becomes the headquarters' primary point of reference.

SECTIONAL PERSPECTIVE

MASTER SITE PLAN

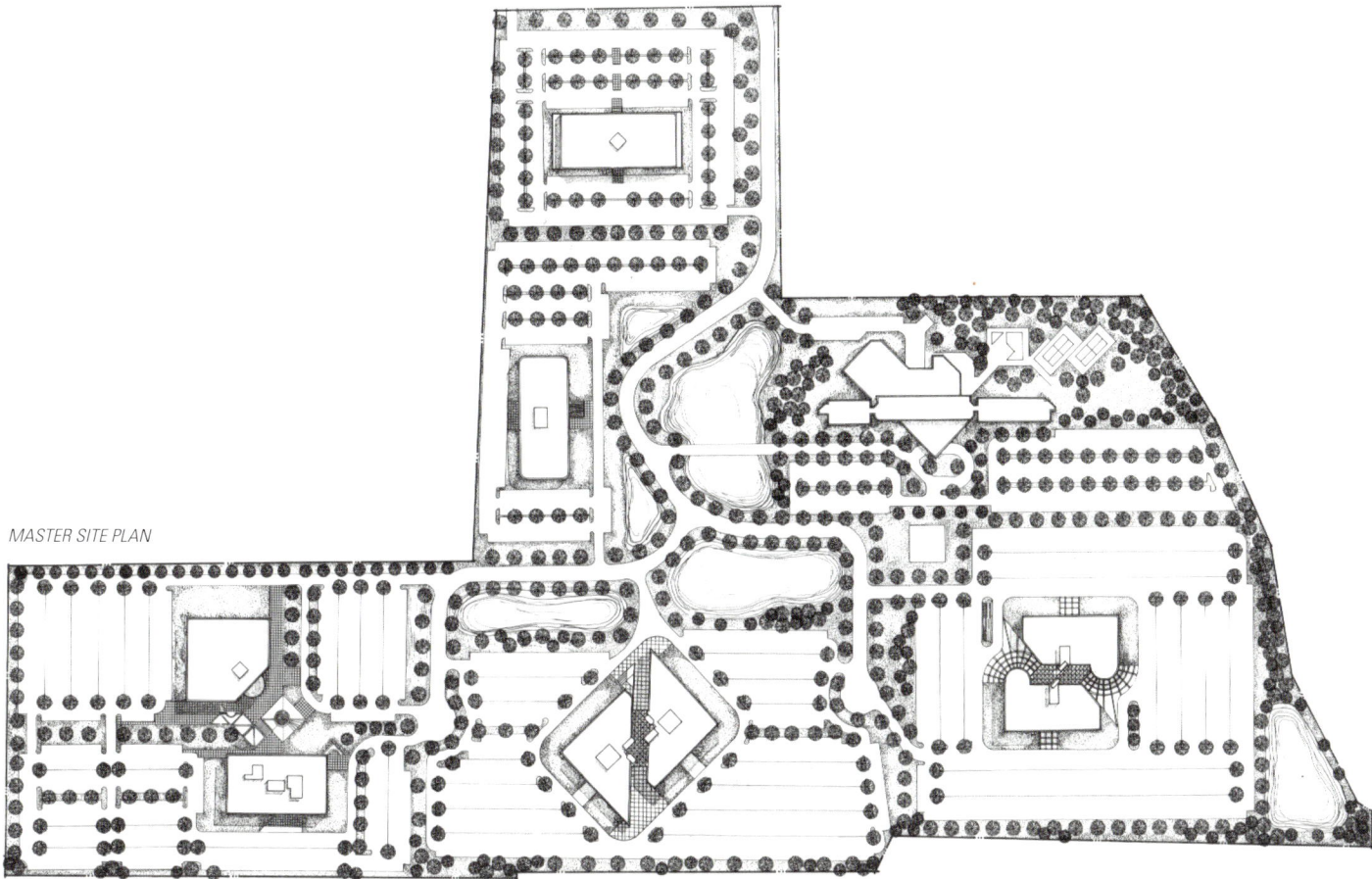

Merrill Lynch Executive Group   Somerset, New Jersey

A challenge was presented to the architect to design an executive center that expressed the corporate identity of Merrill Lynch and could function as two separate entities for future expansion and growth. Situated on a ninety-four-acre corporate office park in central New Jersey, the Executive Center is a gateway to the entire site and acts as a pinwheel which mirrors the adjoining facilities.

The economical and structural purity of a square was manipulated to create a form of simple geometry with multiple function capabilities. By bisecting the square and juxtaposing two triangular configurations, a dynamic tension was formed diagonally bonding triangle and square together. The fissure created between the two halves serves a dual purpose: it is an entry to the building as well as a public space.

In the lobby, stair towers and bridges are subliminal guides to the designated wing as they follow the building's form. The atrium space within the two wings is sheathed both vertically and horizontally by spaceframe and glass, penetrated only by stair and elevator towers expressed on the exterior. Custom-detailed pipe rails, elevator cabs, a vertical planked-plenum ceiling, and state-of-the-art lighting lend elegance to this energetic environment. Two strong sculptures, created from different mediums, announce an innovative environment as one approaches the entry plaza. Exterior strength is communicated through the building's thrusting angular facades.

Steel frame construction enhanced with a composite joist system saved forty percent in costs. This system was custom-designed for the client and became a role model in American joist system technology.

INTERIOR ATRIUM, PERSPECTIVE

According to Merrill Lynch, the vitality and energy of the Executive Center's design has greatly increased employee productivity.

40 and 80 Cuttermill Road   Great Neck, New York

The suburban community of Great Neck, New York, with its close proximity to New York City, is a vital, thriving business peninsula. It is more urban in feeling and progressive in nature than many adjacent townships. On a main avenue in this community, the Spector Group has had the opportunity to design three office buildings and two residential structures.

40 Cuttermill Road is a four-story, 75,000-square-foot structure. Its main axis is accentuated by stairways that are expressed on the exterior of both the front and rear elevations. This treatment provides the floors a sense of privacy for small business users. Parking is on grade and underground.

Entry to 80 Cuttermill Road is through an exterior circular seating and sculpture area. Designed with a strong diagonal axis and multiple setbacks, the building appears to be moving away. Revealed structure forges a relationship with human scale. Innovative lightweight bracing is used in place of steel on the entire structure.

Aluminum exteriors create sleek facades for both structures, in contrast to rough heavy planters and artwork at the main and rear entries. State-of-the-art ambient lighting complements the lobby interior and office cores.

Employee amenities were important for both buildings; plazas, urban landscaping, and artwork encourage employee and visitor participation.

Grumman Data Systems — Brookhaven, New York

A square superimposed on a triangular base yields efficient use of space within Grumman Data Systems. The design for this corporate headquarters exploits the building as an identifiable computer facility by projecting a solid mass beyond the facade plane.

Enclosed forms and voids on the exterior walls reveal functional space beyond. The application of metal panels and continuous glass block together with curved tile stair walls transforms these elements into a graphic, visual art form.

Early discussions of plans for the red exterior stair drew expressions of surprise from design team and client alike. The final scheme manipulates the stairway to the extreme, and the framed opening becomes a metaphor for a work of art.

Dictated by the program, the primary function of computer operations is separated from the secondary function of administrative activities located on the two above-ground levels.

A soaring silver facade points toward the sky, reminiscent of flight – Grumman's signature.

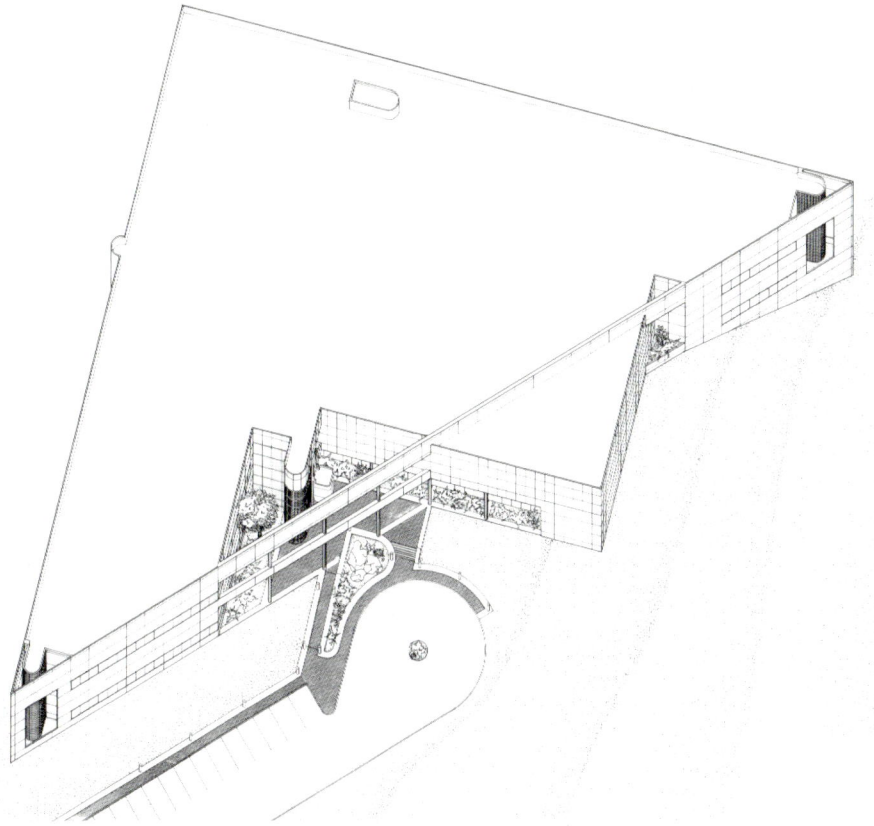

Long Island Savings Bank   Melville, New York

Named for the region it serves, Long Island Savings Bank sought a highly visible headquarters that would express their dedication to the future, while maintaining the strength of traditional values within. The bank sought to project a strong yet approachable environment, sensitive to the surrounding landscape.

An existing two-story structure provided thirty percent of the necessary square footage required in the programming of this headquarters building. A cumbersome column layout and low, varying ceiling heights presented a series of complex design and structural challenges. Through the repetition of detail, emphasis of vertical structure, and stepped terrace configurations, these complexities became assets and resulted in a clear and consistent sense of design unification.

As a visitor enters the main atrium space, greenery and the exterior finish of bright white crystallized glass is carried through; granite paving unites interior and exterior. A cylindrical core of Neoparies, granite, and glass rise from the center of the atrium, allowing the boardroom and executive areas above a view of the atrium architecture. Capped by a skylit dome softened by concentric rings, the atrium space serves as the public zone leading to the main elevator core. The vaulted ceiling above is marked by detail that is carried through to the executive areas.

The main atrium and staff lobby surround visitor and employee alike with water and landscaping on all sides. The two areas act as natural buffers to the neighborhood beyond. A series of diagonal perimeter walls play a key role in allowing the building to meet its environment, as landscapes and private gardens are incorporated into the facade and inner courtyards. Just as shades of blue and green compose the interior environment, the world of nature interacts with the building's exterior, symbolizing the alliance between the bank and the community it serves.

Interpreted as a thematic design element, the sawtooth wall is a functional design solution. On the exterior, it provides multiple window offices for staff; in the cafeteria, it masks an existing double column layout and provides privacy to diners. The administrative assistant workspaces are staggered as well, lending them greater visibility and ease of communication.
— Peter Toh

SP-20-O

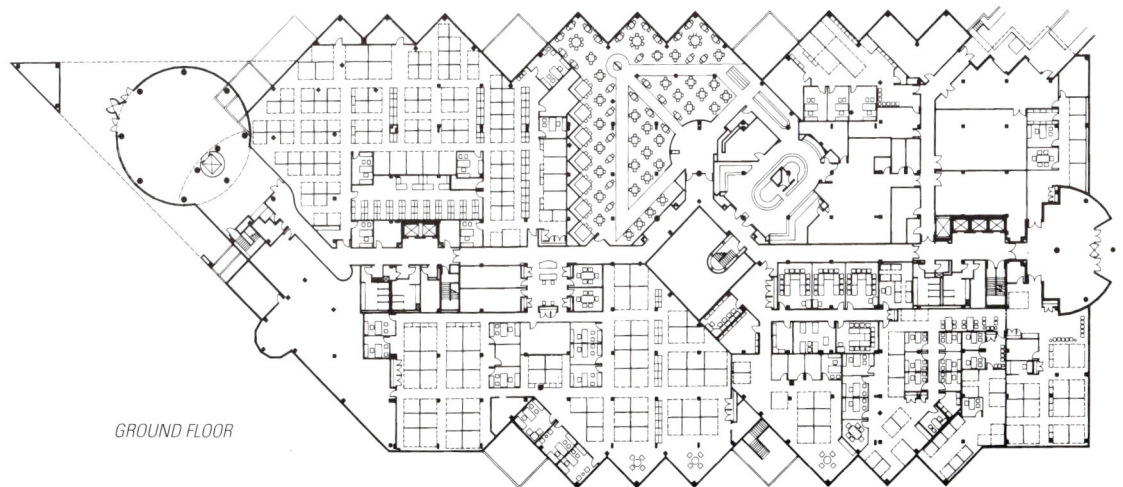

GROUND FLOOR

85

ATRIUM SECTION

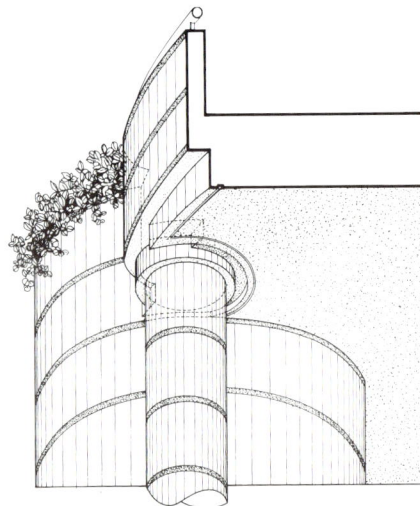

Traditional wood finishes contrast sharply to the sleek Neoparies, each enhancing the other. The charge to communicate strength and security within a modern atmosphere was paramount in the design process.

Metropolis New York, New York

The excitement of planning an entire city block on Manhattan's West Side was the charge engaged upon winning this international design competition. A multitude of challenges and concerns by the owner, planning boards, and community groups came under consideration.

The developers planned to use a pre-existing neoclassical high school as the gateway to a vast mixed-use complex. This complex was to be responsive to its historical neighbors and mindful of many parameters including zoning, set back requirements, height, views, and presence of public space.

The Spector Group presented three schemes to incorporate multifamily housing, offices, retail, and television production studio facilities. The favored scheme featured two mid-rise towers. The 11th Avenue tower, a more fluid form, was defined as the residential tower, located away from the more commercial interests of the avenue. The 10th Avenue office tower, the more rectangular format, reflects its businesslike function. Between the structures are glass atriums, totally transparent, exposing the vitality of flying bridges, retail stores, restaurants, and recreational facilities, which suggest a small town unto itself. The incorporation of public space to be enjoyed year round qualified the project for coveted city bonuses.

Our first high-rise competition...
we won. We now had the
opportunity to look skyward.

Ivy Tower   New York, New York

Between West 44th and West 45th Street, an area in midtown Manhattan dominated by alumni clubs, a site was acquired adjacent to the landmark New York Yacht Club. The plan for Ivy Tower is organized around an alumni club community, with spaces designed for families to attend conferences, enjoy the facilities, and reside while visiting Manhattan. The Harvard Club and a turn-of-the-century hotel are located nearby.

A double tower concept was proposed for this community, yielding 500,000 square feet at forty stories above grade, two floors below grade, and parking for fifty cars at one floor below grade. One street entry leads to the College Club, and a five-story open atrium leads directly to the first tower. Eight floors of club facilities, a two-floor fitness center, and a twenty-eight-floor residential space make up the first tower. The second entry also opens to a five-story atrium, which leads to a forty-story office tower.

Surrounded on both sides by landmark buildings, Ivy Tower's first eight floors reflect their context. The upper floors are then stepped back, to create the five-story atriums and to maintain a more human scale. They adapt classical design principles in modern terms, suggesting new architectural direction in the immediate area. Manipulation of adjacent properties produced an efficient use of the allowable FAR.

44TH STREET ELEVATION

45TH STREET ELEVATION

Ivy Tower expresses classical design principals in modern terms.

Roslyn Highlands Firehouse   Roslyn, New York

While the Roslyn Firehouse Company required technology of the twenty-first century, the municipality requested a building that respected its historic environment. In response to a rolling site and a progressive urban renewal plan, a synergy resulted between building orientation, circulation, materials, texture, and color. With careful attention to budget, operational needs, and a highly visible location, the design solution bridges the firehouse's historical role with its functional layout. The winner of the esteemed Award for Design Excellence from the Masonry Institute, this firehouse incorporates textures of warm-toned brick accented by traditional fire engine red details.

The program's comprehensive design solution transformed the firehouse interior and separated the functional apparatus room from the administrative areas. A curved east wall, carved into the building and placed over the square form, creates a precise division. An aggregate of contextual components, the firehouse embraces the fragmented elements of its surroundings.

When you're a kid, your most precious toys are a fire engine and a red wagon. When asked to design a firehouse, I was a kid again.
— Michael Harris Spector

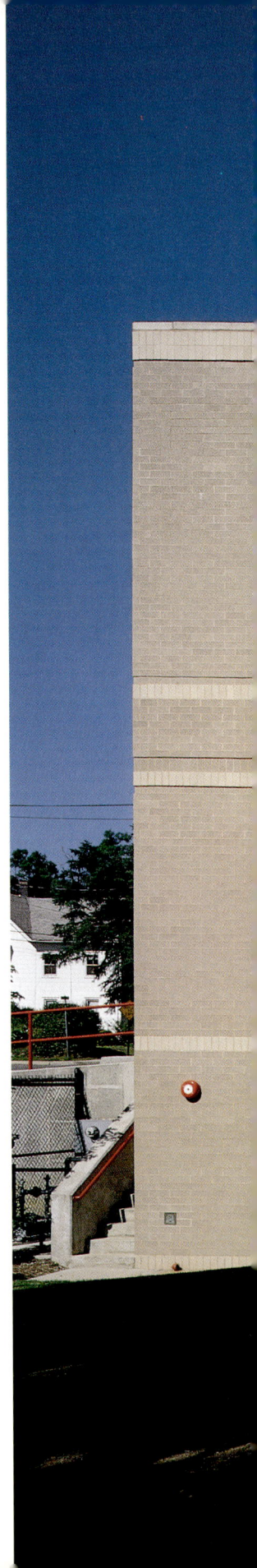

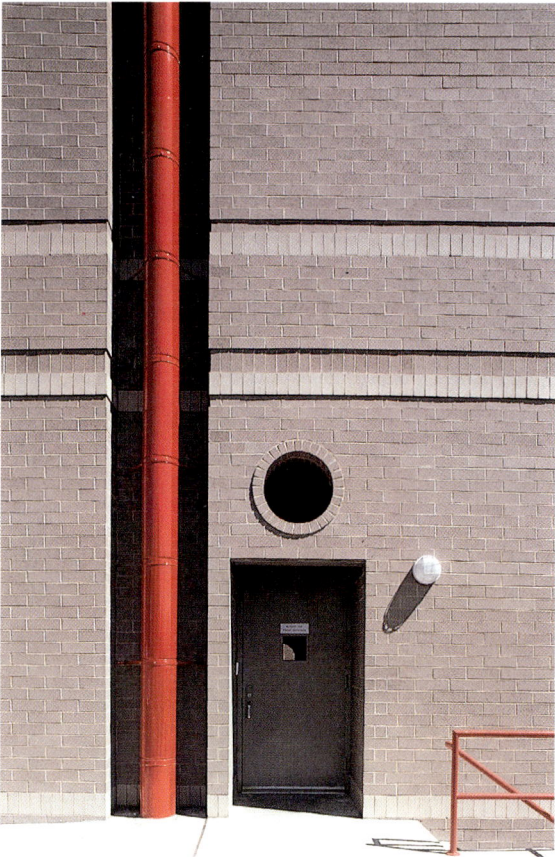

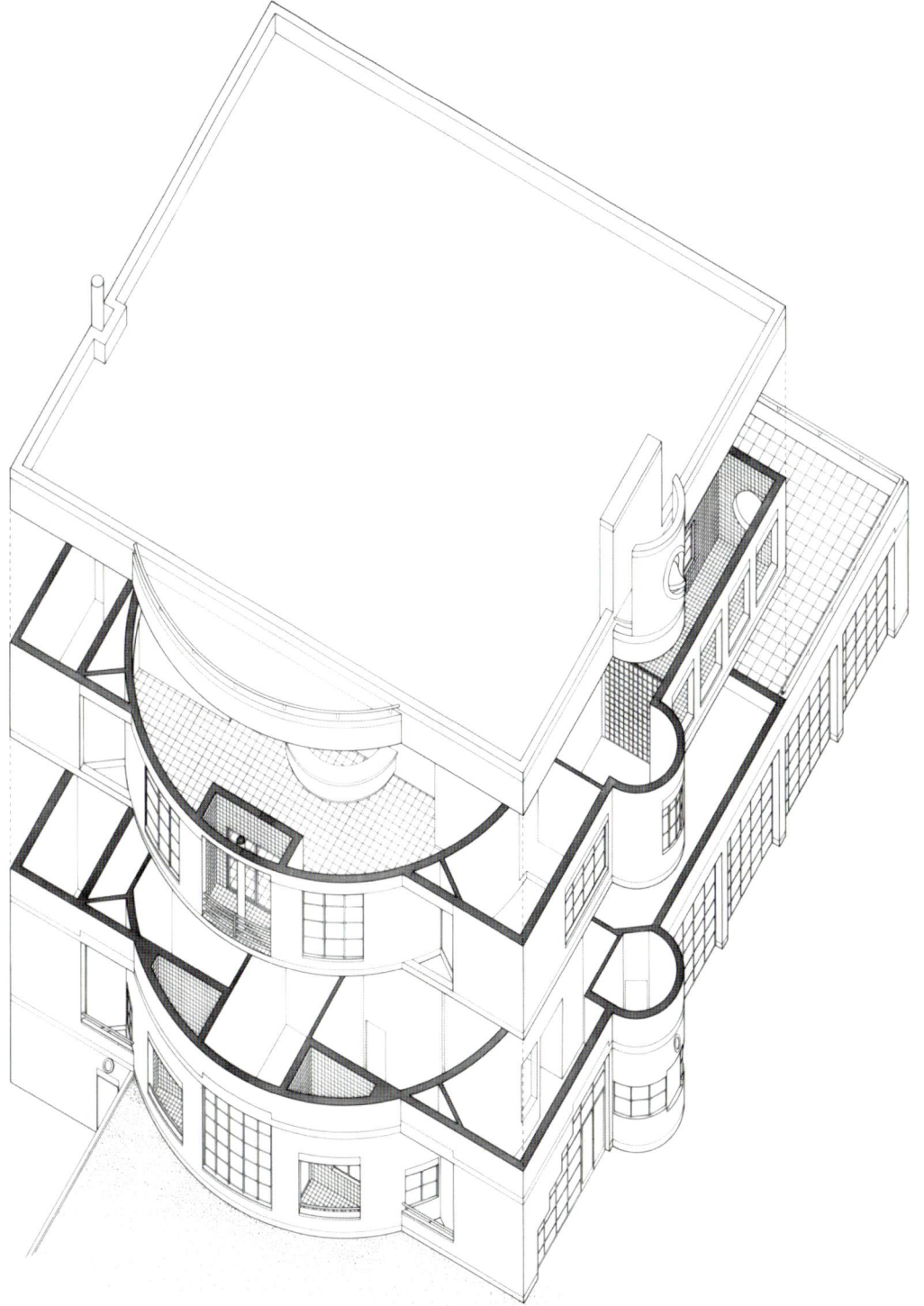

AXONOMETRIC

Long Island University   Greenvale, New York

Analysis of the campus environment and of campus circulation patterns helped determine this building's design. To establish an image that is new but in harmony with the rest of the two-hundred-acre campus, a combination of masonry materials is used for the exterior building pods. Dormitory entrances that stand opposite one another create a common courtyard in between. The existing circulation pattern has been redirected to encourage a lively interaction between new and old. A screen at each entry defines transitional space between the common courtyard and entry while color on the four frontal facades gives each pod an individual identity. The building mass, evolved from a study of student traffic patterns and an understanding of the communality of university experience, is linked at the lower level to provide comfortable flow of community and pedestrian activity.

Integration and assimilation is furthered within each unit; there are seven students to a suite, each sharing four bedrooms and living spaces. Suites are grouped four per floor, three stories high, forming a cluster. Each cluster has its own separate entrance, lounge, and bathroom facility. The lower levels contain common areas including computer lab, meeting rooms, and laundry.

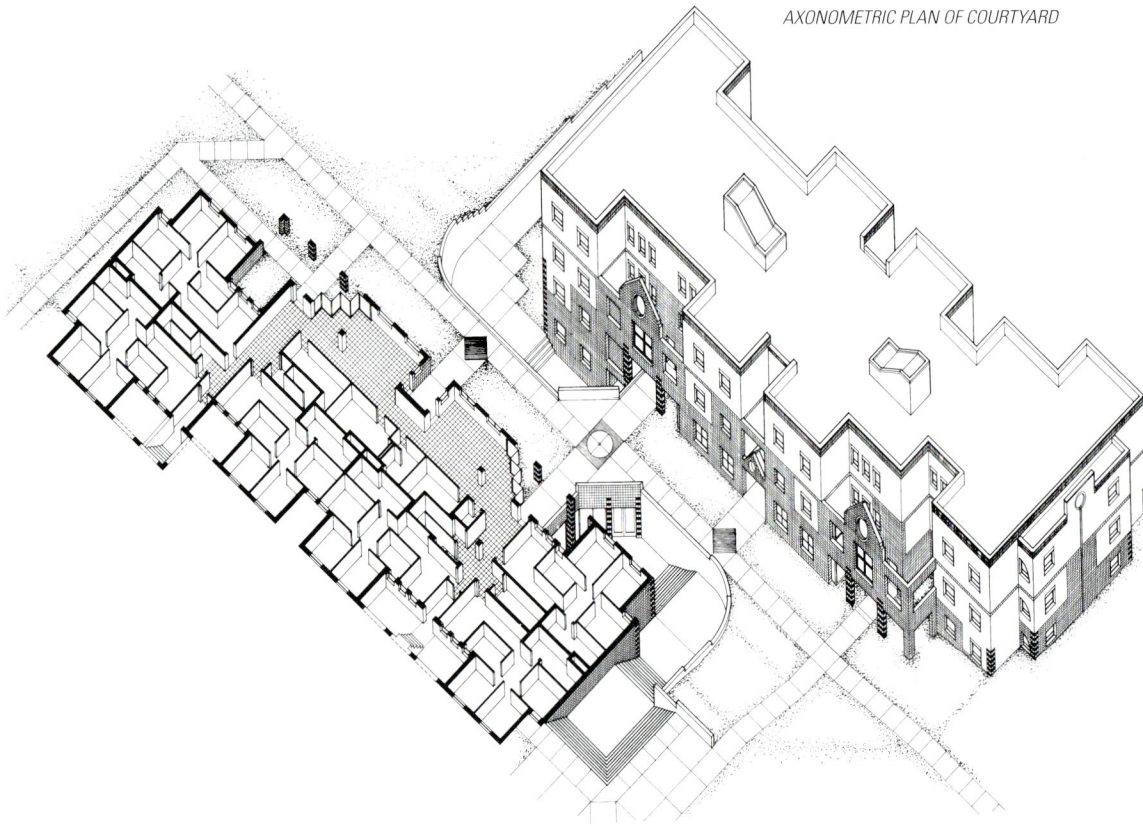

CONTEXT ANALYSIS

Labels within the drawing:

CHAPEL

RIGGS HALL

POST HALL

BROOKVILLE HALL

GENERAL PARKING

BEDROOM

LIVING ROOM

BEDROOM

BEDROOM

BEDROOM

STORAGE

KITCHEN

LOUNGE

Layered facades between dormitory
and courtyard define transitional
space; colorful glazed masonry
further defines each entryway.

Ronald McDonald House   New York, New York

Dedicated to establishing a healing environment and a facility sensitive to the emotional needs of families, the Ronald McDonald House was designed as a home away from home for families whose children are struggling with life-threatening illnesses. Complementing the brownstone context of the residential neighborhood, the avenue facade of the building is composed of precast concrete and granite. The elegant entry of gray-and rose-colored granite reflects warmth and strength and represents a haven of safety. Combined with glass, the facade presents an open and inviting environment.

Once inside Ronald McDonald House, families are greeted with the life-affirming symbols of light, air, water, and greenery. A fireplace glows at the heart of the building, in the center of a five-story "Great Room." Fabric and natural wood finishes allow the warmth of home to flow through the interior. In recognition of the common experiences each family shares, open space invites interaction throughout the public areas. Often, sets of parents can be found sharing meals, concerns, and the day's events. Two-bedroom suites for parents and siblings adjoin kitchen facilities.

A 5,000-square-foot play area spreads out below the rising atrium and exposed balconies. A media room, game room, and playground encourage motor coordination and provide a haven from anxiety.

73RD STREET CONTEXT SKETCH

The unique rooftop garden has been nicknamed "parktop." The three-story, glass-enclosed rooftop atrium is environmentally controlled. Parents and children can walk through a naturally landscaped garden within the protection of the facility. It is a peaceful place to relax and reflect.

Maimonides Medical Center Brooklyn, New York

Maimonides Medical Center is a 705-bed hospital providing multiple services in the Brooklyn area. It functions as a community hospital, tertiary care center, and an institute for graduate education. During the past twenty years, the institution's programs and facilities have grown rapidly. Thus, a program was developed by the Spector Group to create a proposed architectural master plan. This solution will allow Maimonides to move into the twenty-first century as a medical leader by providing state-of-the-art diagnostic functions in a user-friendly environment, responsive to the needs of both patient and physician.

Departmental blocking and stacking and enhancement of horizontal and vertical transportation traffic patterns will create the most efficient and workable atmosphere. All patient- and visitor-related service areas and departments will be upgraded and inefficient service departments expanded. As well, a new facilities master plan will prepare the institution for increased ambulatory care.

All clinical campus facilities, such as faculty offices and educational administration affairs, will be in one contiguous area, fostering integration between medical education and clinical care. A new interior spine, or "Main Street," will provide horizontal circulation for all outpatient and inpatient functions and for the new 1,000-car parking garage. Strategically placed elevator cores will control and improve vertical transportation throughout the facility.

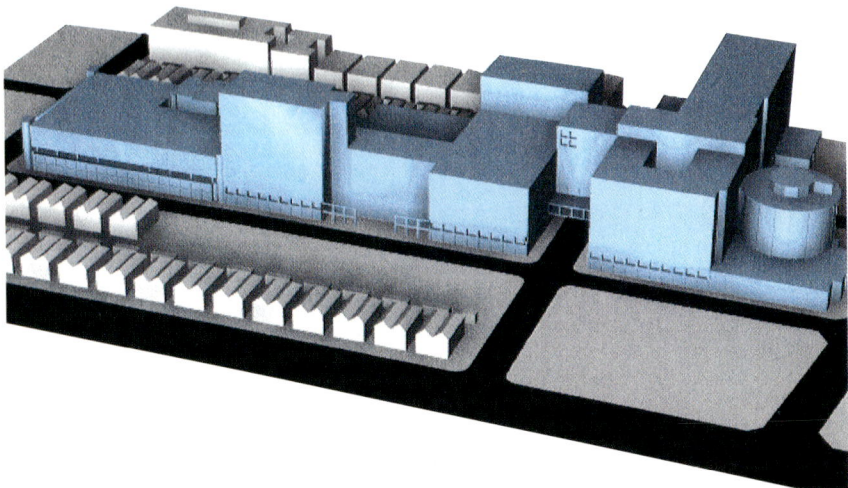

State-of-the-art ambulatory care is the prominent role of the Medical Arts Building.

Horizon One   Hollywood, Florida

Responding to expansion in the Florida real estate market, the Spector Group designed Horizon One as a speculative office building that would meet the demands of Florida's sophisticated new breed of corporate tenants and commercial real estate developers. Situated on a highly visible site adjoining the Florida Turnpike, Horizon One's striking facades of green reflective and vision glass command the attention of potential users and passersby. Exterior red balconies accent the distinctive curving facades and highlight a perfectly symmetrical form.

The headquarters' structural purity was extremely cost-effective, and these design elements also play strongly to their tropical climate. As the architecture mirrors the environment in its reflective facade, outdoor balconies provide additional meeting, dining, and break-away locations. Custom tiling for the balconies, lobby, and plazas display a distinctive attention to detail.

The long access drive is flanked by reflecting pools and fountains on both sides, while extensive landscaping creates a parklike environment. The landscaping and public plaza extend into the two-story atrium, connecting the main entrance and the rear employee entrance in a well-organized, transitional manner. Paving design in and out of the atrium celebrates the entrance through pattern and color.

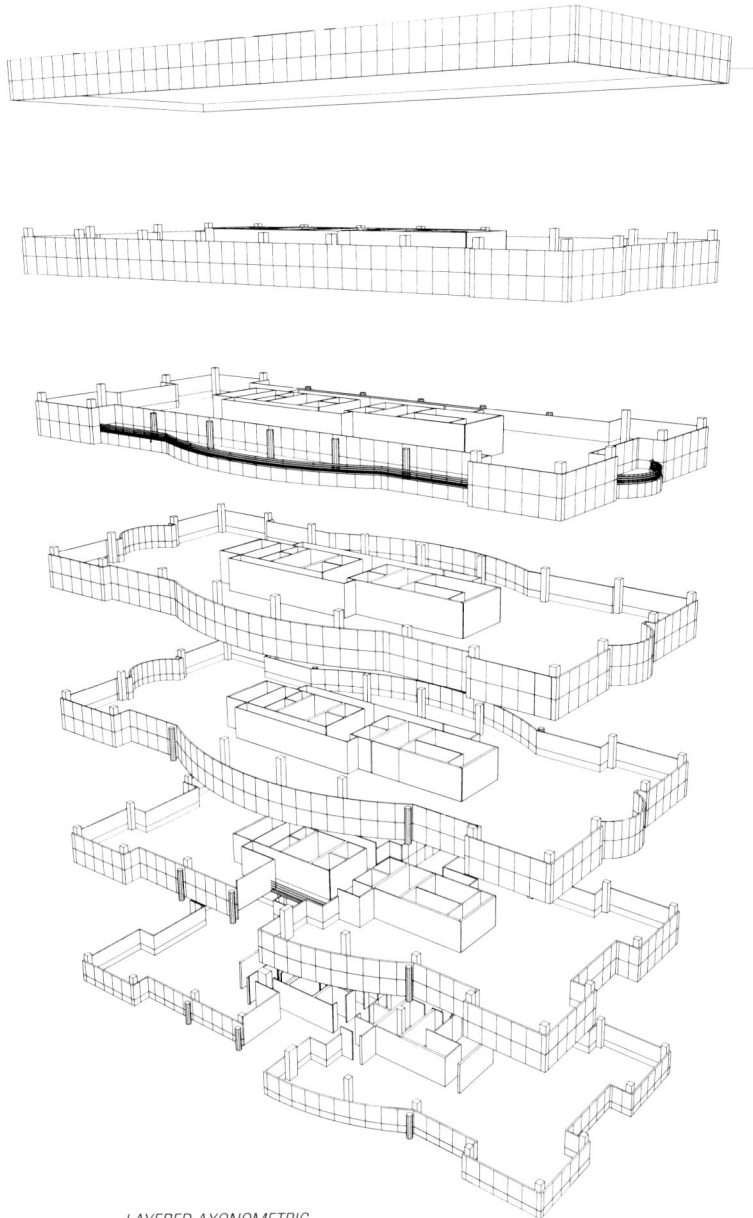

LAYERED AXONOMETRIC

Curved balconies highlight the symmetry and break the massing of the glass facade.

Fleet Bank Corporate Headquarters Melville, New York

As the first to be completed and the most visible of four buildings in this corporate center, Fleet Bank's headquarters responds to present needs and promises flexibility for the future. Boldly sited, the building is designed to project an image of strength and endurance to both business and consumer clientele.

From the main crossroads, passersby view the winged, blue and silver glass-banded headquarters set amidst a rolling green lawn. Twin four-story rectangles, 105,000 square feet each, are joined by a 7,000-square-foot, 45-foot-high atrium topped with a barrel-vaulted skylight. Fleet Bank occupies one wing and, until expansion space is required, leases the second. Dual entrances into the atrium with adjacent entries into each wing ensure controlled circulation.

The atrium is the only area where the two wings of the building converge. In addition to a restaurant, a branch bank, access to a retail center, and underground parking can be found within. This space encourages gathering and activity for employees and visitors as they pass through the building. The terrazzo floor patterns, light from the skylight above, and natural greenery are characteristic of an open meeting square.

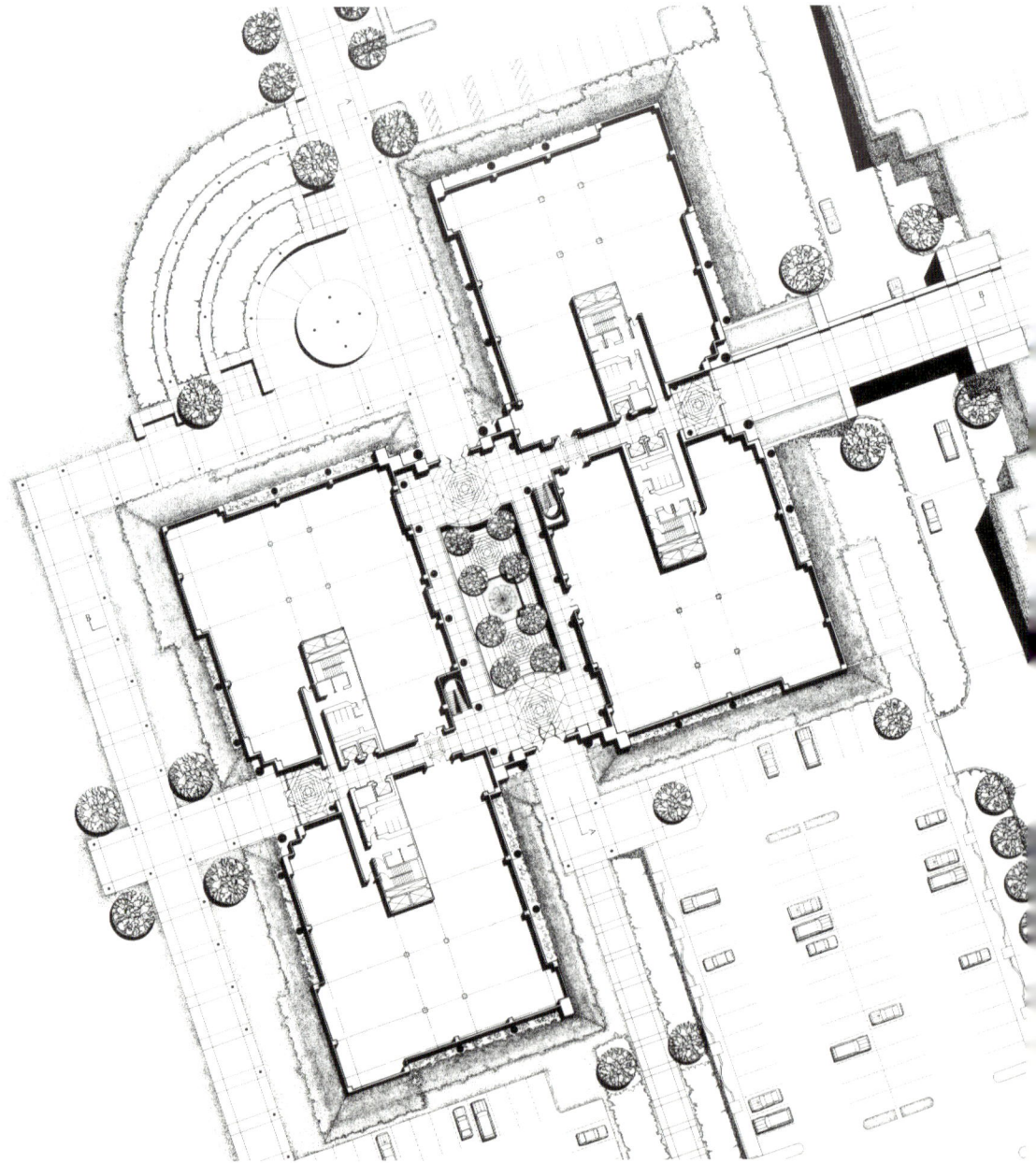

Key Bank Headquarters   Islandia, New York

Key Bank at the Islandia Pavilion is the first corporate office project planned for this newly established hamlet. Eager for growth-oriented companies, the township sought a facility that would attract Fortune 500 corporate users to the area and would offer a wide range of services and amenities. They wanted to set a precedent for future development.

The building is a triangular structure designed to suit its highly visible, irregular hilltop site. This 167,000-square-foot facility features multicolored glass facades. Natural shades of rose and aquamarine glass shine in a spectrum of color that varies through the course of a day.

Within the structure, a five-story, seventy-five-foot-high atrium envelopes a multilevel space defined by granite, landscaping, and color. Bridges and balconies line the perimeter and are anchored by a glass-enclosed circular elevator core. A gabled glass roof lets in natural light while water cascading below creates an environment of energy and motion, of corporate quality and productivity. Exposed trusswork and ventilation ducts impart the essence of this intelligent, high-technology facility.

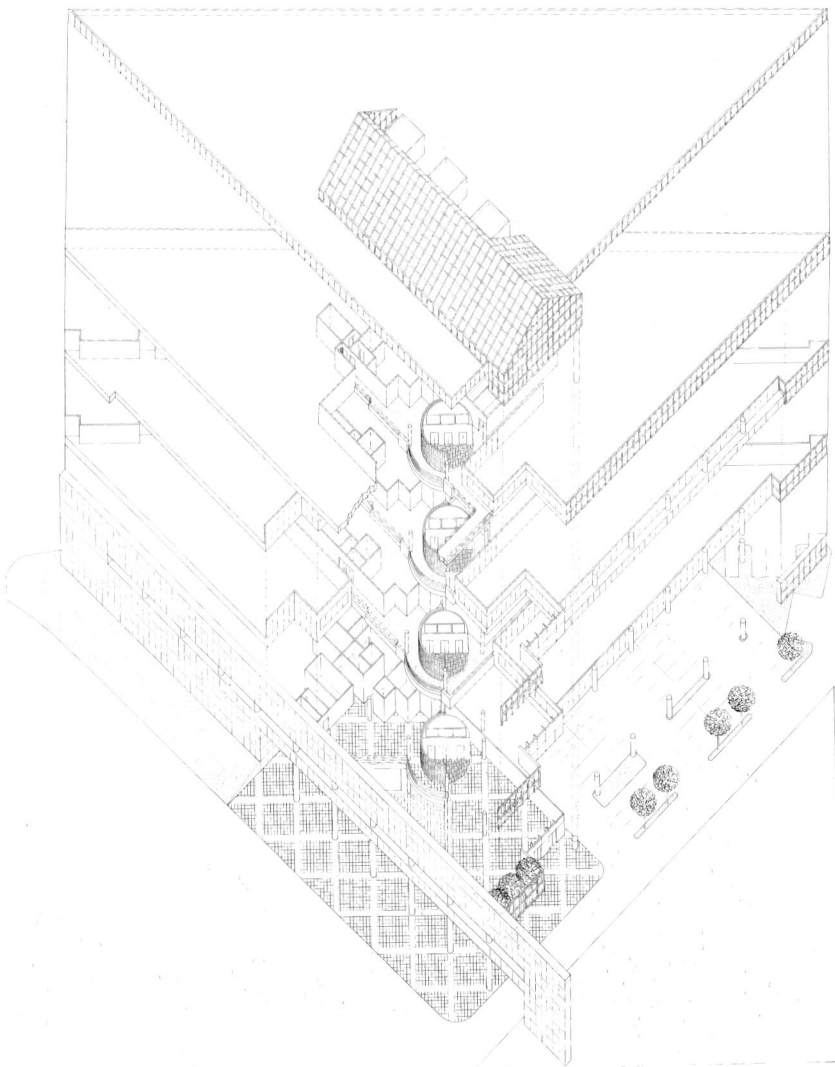

An extended southern facade creates a vehicular entry.

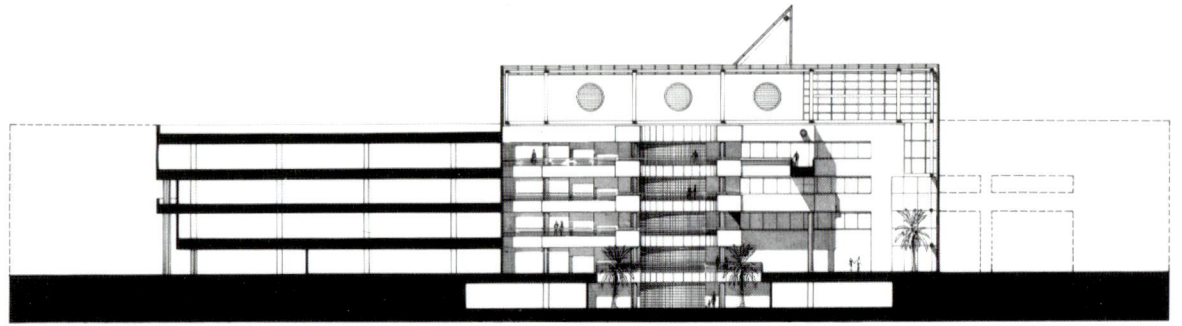

118

Multilevel space creates
an environment of energy
and motion.

General Accident Insurance Company Melville, New York

Highly responsive to the surrounding architecture and environs, General Accident Insurance Company's regional headquarters overlooks Long Island's two major crossroads. Designed to interact with two adjacent headquarter buildings, landscaping, vast public plazas, and underground parking link the three structures together.

The 157,000-square-foot headquarters curves in a 240-foot radius. A fifth-story mechanical penthouse bisects the curve, and steps down to four-, three-, two-, and one-story elements, creating a fanlike pattern. Within this arc of stone and glass, protected gardens, fountains, and plazas surround the entryways.

While the structure presents a conservative image, it also conveys a futuristic orientation and imparts a feeling of security and depth. Glass and granite facades suggest precious facets to be guarded by this corporation's tangible structure and image of reliability. Located at the pinnacle of the building, the corporate boardroom's unusual triangular exterior cantilevers over the atrium.

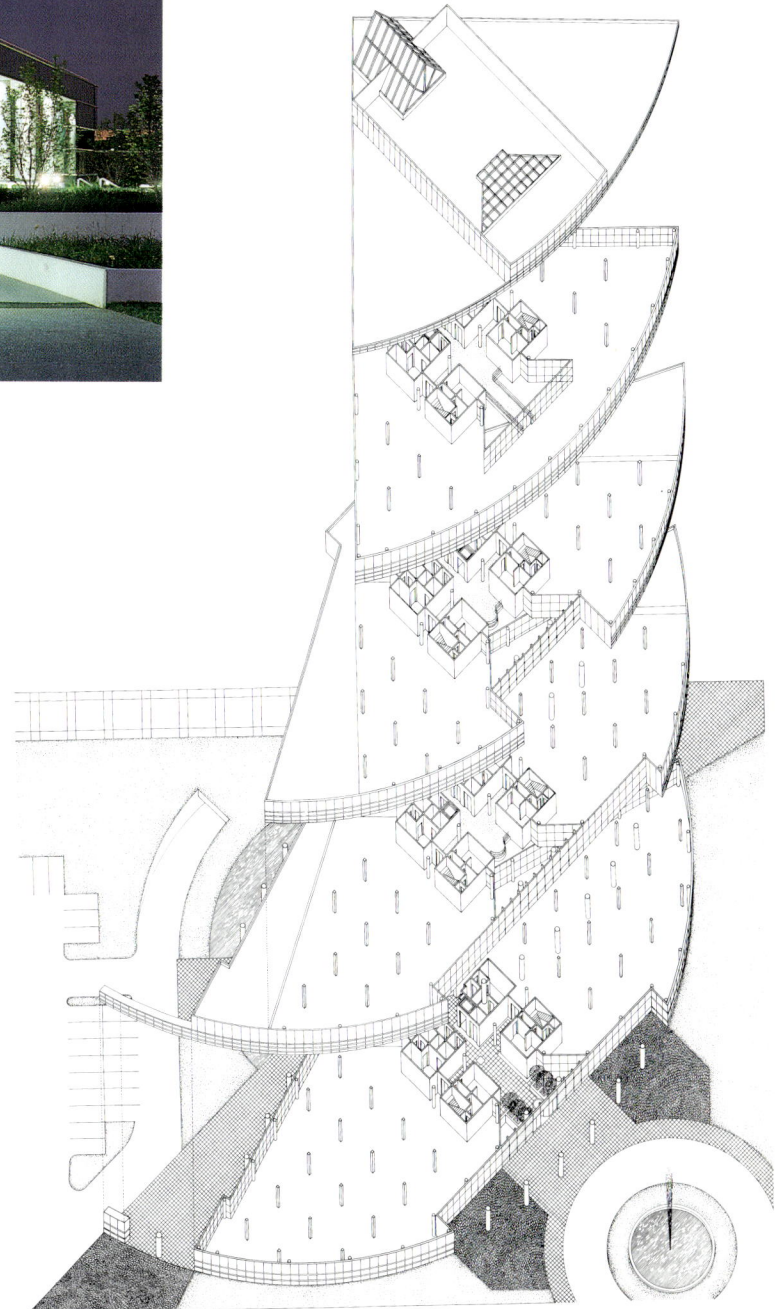

Granite and glass continue
to the atrium spaces and
introduce this protected
environment.

Country Glen Center   Carle Place, New York

Built before World War II, and once used to process aircraft, the buildings at Country Glen have undergone a series of renovations. They stand amidst a high-density commercial area, dominated by an aging one million-square-foot regional mall. The adaptive reuse of this industrial complex into a community-oriented retail center makes a vibrant contrast with the environment and its manufacturing origins.

The introduction of Country Glen Center brings a twenty-first century power center to this suburban region. Amassing 270,000 square feet, the Center is a celebration of space, dimension, and vitality. Five towers provide visual accents and orientation for the tenant; the architecture incorporates color and faceted skylights to let bright, natural light into covered pedestrian walkways. On the perimeter, white fiberglass columns with red accent banding support tiled "billboards." Clearly spaced signage joins the colorful parade.

Though all of the retail space is on one level, pyramid-shaped skylights suggest vertical and horizontal depth. Colorfully landscaped plazas filled with greenery, flags, and water surround the retail outlets and complement this festive, parklike environment.

A breath of fresh air. – Mel Simon

River Run Community — Ocean City, Maryland

Across the bay from the resort community of Ocean City, Maryland, the St. Martins River in Worcester County will play host to River Run. This proposed luxury, 408-unit development affords each townhome or condominium a water or golf course view. Although its setting is rural and picturesque, the project represents one of the largest residential communities in the northeast. Sited on 258 acres, River Run has extensive recreational facilities, including an 18-hole Gary Player Signature golf course, six championship tennis courts, a health and fitness spa, and indoor and outdoor Olympic-sized swimming pools. A 180-slip marina, clubhouse, and restaurant are also planned.

The residences at River Run will be grouped in clusters of two, three, and four, with each cluster illustrating a unique architectural design solution. By creating an illusion of grand manor homes, the project's side-by-side arrangement of townhouses respects this historic neighborhood. Thematic design elements include stepped, gridded windows, dual chimneys, and elegant stairways. Some entryways pass through a rear courtyard, following a series of portals through to gardens. In master planning River Run, the concept was to create homes whose vaulted ceilings, skylights, courtyards, and expansive vistas would unite them with the surrounding landscape.

I've only been playing golf for six years and now have the opportunity to tee off with Gary Player.
– Michael Harris Spector

Century Condominiums   Great Neck, New York

When a former bedroom community becomes a concentrated business center, a proliferation of multifamily housing usually follows. The task of creating an affordable and unique "oasis" in the storm of a bustling town's prosperity was the challenge Century Condominiums presented.

Collaboration among architect, developer, and municipality lead to a well-defined set of objectives for the design process. A high-density project—58 units on a single acre—was desired. Another challenge was the height and mass of the complex as it relates to the immediate environment and the overall architectural characteristics of the community. In addition, design had to consider the long, narrow site, noise generated by passing traffic, and the limited opportunities for landscaped views.

A series of earthtone sculptural curves are presented to the avenue and define the front facade of this two-building complex. While the curves form outdoor balconies for individual units, they also set the building back from the avenue to maintain a sense of human scale. Abundant greenery further softens the exterior. As the front facade parallels the avenue, the two buildings parallel each other and create a courtyard in between. A needed focal point within the semiurban environment, this grassy inner sanctum, which contains a sculpture garden with plantings and space for relaxation, draws the two structures together.

The condominiums' sculptural forms carry throughout the residence. An arching entryway, spiral lobby staircase, and cylindrical elevator core repeat the building's graceful curves.

CONTEXT DIAGRAM

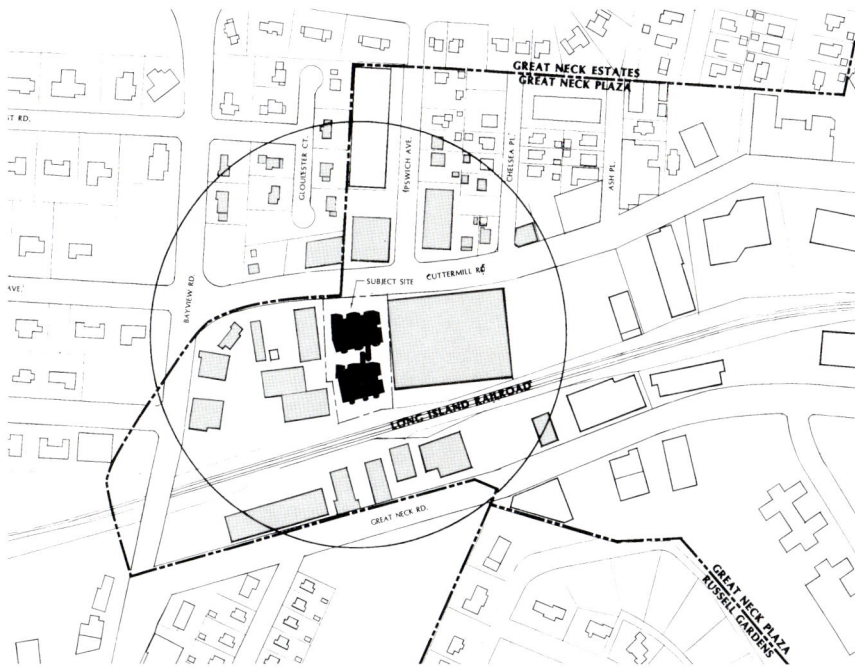

Hewlett-Woodmere School District Hewlett, New York

Due to increased enrollment in the 1980s, the Hewlett-Woodmere School District undertook a consolidation program to merge four elementary schools into two, convert a former elementary school into an early childhood center, merge two junior high schools into a middle school, and expand a high school.

This multiphased project began with the oldest building in the district, a vintage 1929 elementary school. The work involved new construction, renovation, capital improvements, and site work. Information was gathered through in-depth interviews with school administrators, staff members, faculty, and the Board of Education. The resulting report was then used to develop the overall scope of the renovation project.

Fulfilling a requirement of "historic preservation with modernization," the school was transformed into an environment where light, space, color, and resources are plentiful. Some of the original wooden floors and decorative antique lighting fixtures remain, while each of the twenty-six classrooms received six new computer stations equipped for fiber-optic networking. A previously dark basement was excavated to increase ceiling height and let in natural light. A spacious art room, new lunchroom, and modern kitchen were added to this level as well.

The original 1929 clock, which once controlled all the passing bells in the school, now keeps time in the main office.

A two-story expansion in the U-shaped courtyard creates space for offices, computer and resource rooms, and a new library.

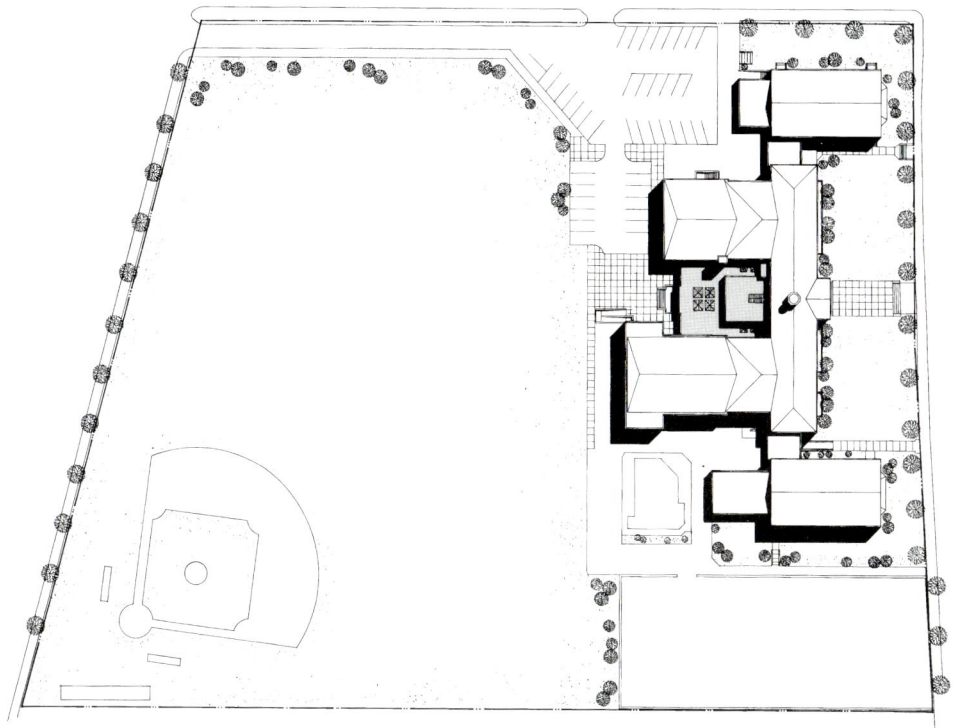

Woodbury Jewish Center Woodbury, New York

A group of young families formed a congregation and chose to build a synagogue in a community where none existed before. Their goal was to assimilate their traditional values with contemporary ideals. The Woodbury Jewish Center was designed to serve as a place of learning and worship, with areas for education and religious services. A catering facility was also included in the program.

The Center's main entrance is set on a diagonal within a prow-shaped spaceframe/porte cochere. Congregation members and guests enter a lobby which accesses all functional areas in the Center. Continuing along a diagonal axis is the entry to the 400-seat sanctuary and a 150-foot aisle leading to the bimah and ark areas. Two stories in height, glass block on the sanctuary's exterior walls maximizes natural light and views of nature. A Star of David is suspended over the ark and bimah area. Outside, a 46-foot-high, spaceframe structure ascends skyward from the corner of the building, further defining this religious symbol.

A skylit galleria along the building's front elevation leads guests from the lobby to the 8,400-square-foot formal banquet hall. This 120-foot-long space parallels the length of the banquet hall and can be used as a pre-function area for private affairs. A stairway in the lobby and a separate exterior stair provide entry to the lower level, where classrooms, offices, a library, and a small chapel are located.

Traditional masonry, contemporary architectural forms, and elements such as glass block, skylights and spaceframe, present a strong, progressive image to the community.

Computer Associates Headquarters Islandia, New York

The philosophy of the complete corporate campus was heartily embraced in this region as client and architect revealed their 1.4 million-square-foot master plan. The design of phase one of the three-phase project incorporates flexibility for future expansion of staff and corporate services as well as multiple employee functions and amenities. The interior is efficient with a layout that fosters interaction between groups and individual staff members. The building's architectural design is a centralized and unifying envelope with an exterior form that expresses technology and a sense of location and community.

Test layouts of multiple functional groups, including security and different time zone operations within the corporate complex, were analyzed. Relationships between the active areas (working, educational, social functions) and passive areas (warehousing and dormitory) were studied and sited accordingly. In the final design plan, functional spaces were organized into groups, then juxtaposed on an east-west axis. These sectors clarify the interior circulation and define exterior massing.

The facility's two-story western sector houses a fitness center, printing facilities, and space for warehousing, marketing, and distribution. Within the center operations module, a seven-hundred-seat cafeteria opens onto an interior courtyard, with terraces for conferences and dining. The eastern module provides a training center, dormitory, and daycare center.

Continuity is attained by a clearly defined "Main Street" passageway along the south elevation. The street provides easy access to all Computer Associates user groups and encourages interaction between departments. The northern elevation dedicates a parallel passageway to streamlining service functions. These corridors clearly define the building edges, provide a sense of location, and create a coherent composition of operations.

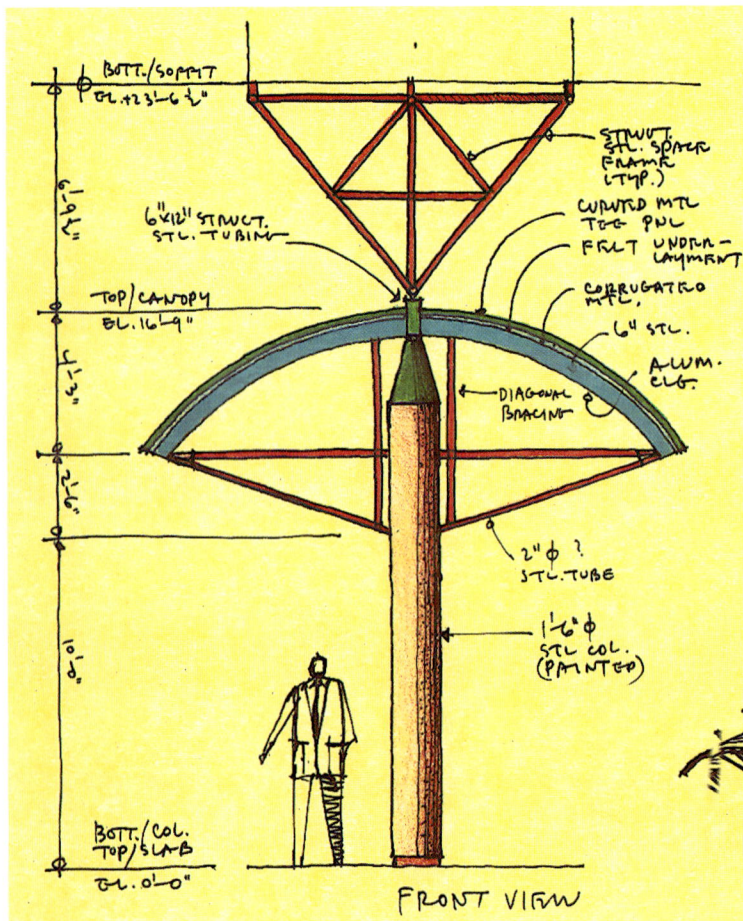

The headquarters' pristine, functional facade demands a distinct main entry. A vibrant canopy is intriguing and offers protection under its umbrellalike structure.

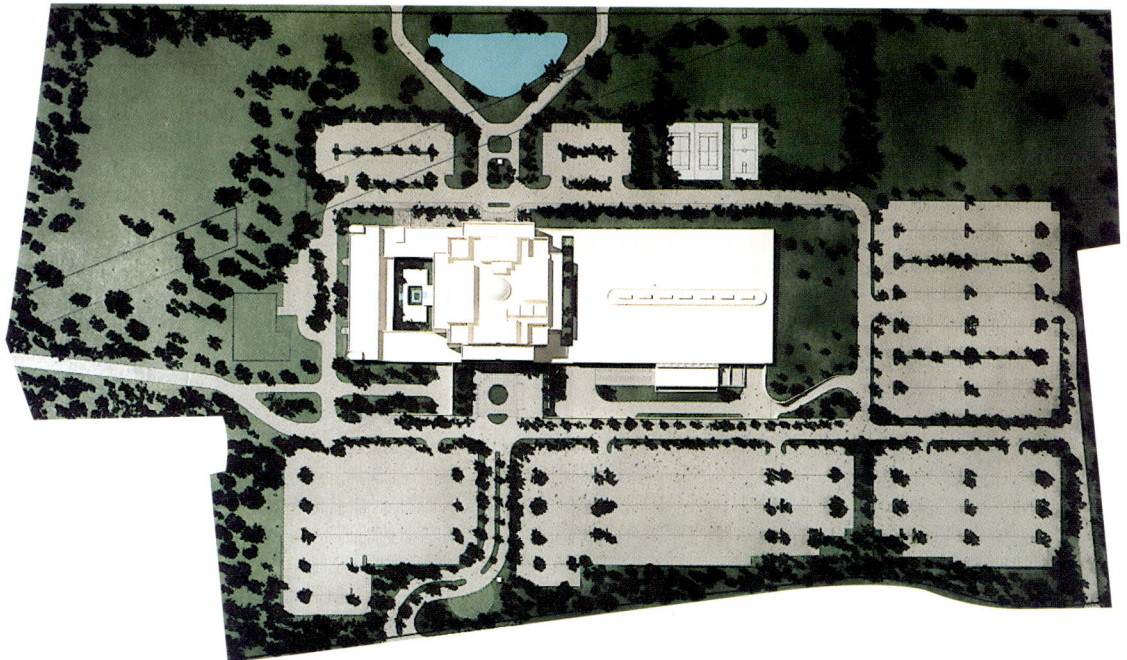

*We envision a building that reflects our
technology and an environment that supports
our energy.* — Charles Wang, Chairman

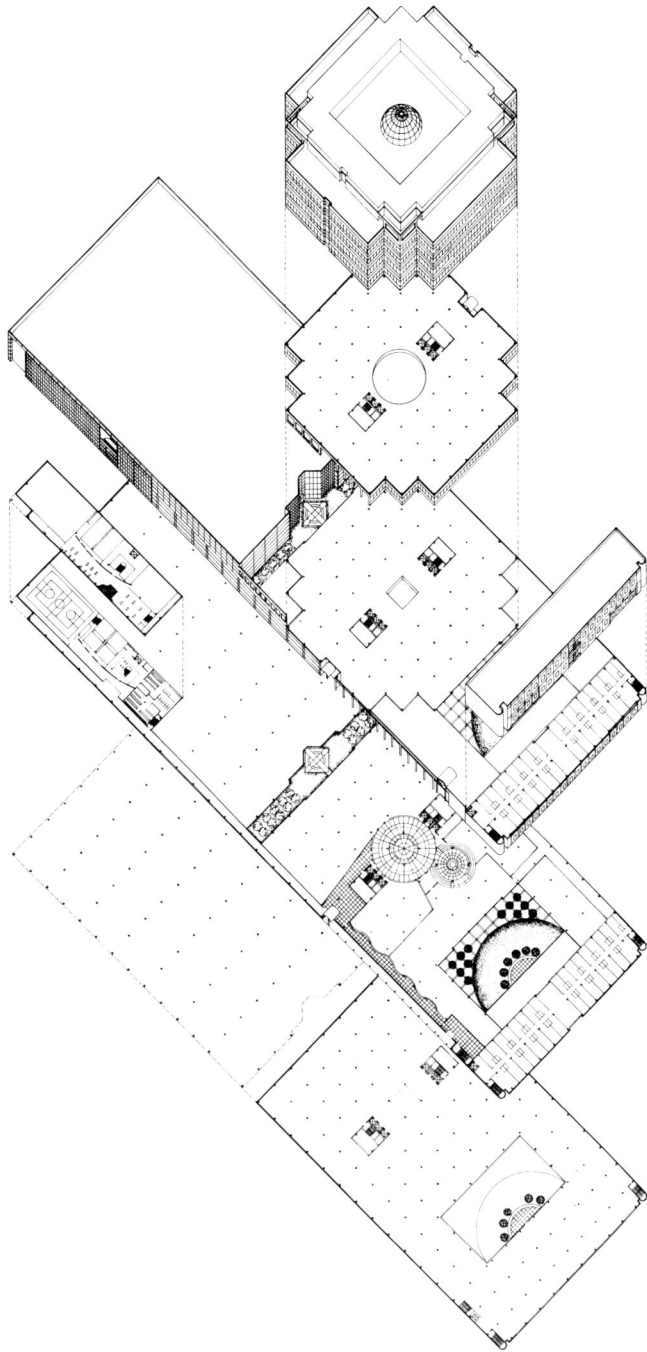

The center module, composed of operations, general offices, and a six-story atrium, serves as a space where staff can visually communicate with each other.

Temple Judea Holocaust Resource Center   Manhasset, New York

The Temple Judea Holocaust Resource Center is a proposed center for learning, reflection, and remembrance. Wedged into a grassy knoll on the north side of an existing temple, the planned structure will employ brick and limestone—materials used throughout Europe. A black granite reflecting pool will serve as a backdrop for the story of the most unsettling, indeed evil result of twentieth-century nationalism and prejudice—Hitler's systematic extermination of the Jewish people.

The structure will consist of a square intersecting a pie-shaped section within a circular plan. The circular flow punctuated with strong geometric forms will create an inviting, yet serious environment for visitors. Two entrances, one for public use and one for the adjacent school, will converge into the Hall of Commandments. Low-vaulted and dimly lit, the hallway will contain ten penetrating stone pylons, representing each of the Ten Commandments. Narrow sections of glass between the pylons will allow minimal light to enter this transitional space and give a brief glimpse of the black granite reflecting pool. Names, places, and events will be engraved in the reflecting pool.

In homage to the strength and dedication of Jewish people to their religious heritage, an Ark will be placed at the center of the building, the point from which all other elements radiate. The Bimah will be visible from any point within the structure.

Within the square section of the building, an exhibit area will be located in adjacent corners, with sections of glass block for daylight illumination. At the exit, a descending mosaic wall serving as a children's memorial will contain ceramic tiles from the United States Holocaust Memorial Museum in Washington D.C. as well as those created by local school students.

This building will not be easy to look at. Nor will it be comfortable to be inside. And because its theme is so important, there is a risk of overestimating the importance of its design. No architecture can fully embrace all that happened during the Holocaust. But the erection of this facility will foster learning in our children. The knowledge they gain can then be passed down to their children. Above all, remembrance is the key.

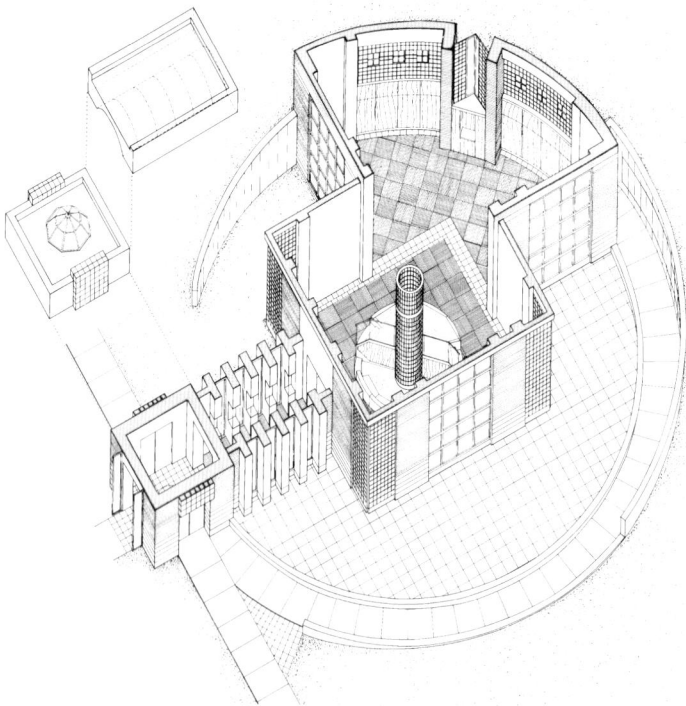

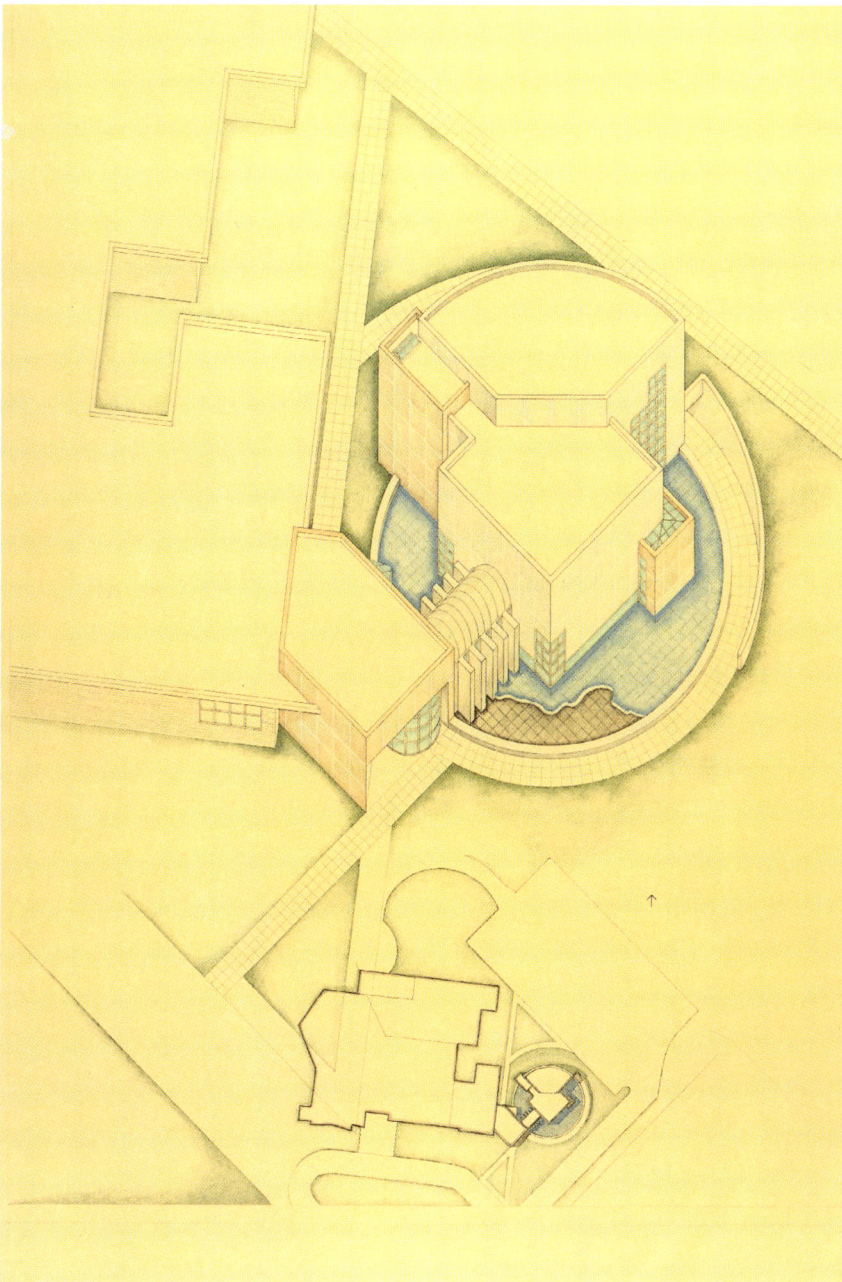

DESIGN ELEVATION PROGRESSION

147

Chase Manhattan Bank Plaza   New York, New York

The prestigious, international atmosphere of Chase Manhattan Plaza is the location of this 25,000-square-foot client reception center. Conference rooms, varying in size from 200 to 700 square feet, occupy the perimeter zone. Interior core space contains open reception areas and break-out rooms.

Transitional furnishings include high-back leather chairs and upholstered lounge chairs. Mahogany and cherry veneers were selected for custom-designed conference tables, desks, and wall coverings. Intersecting bands of green marble floor serve as a border and define carpeted seating areas. The strength and distinction of wood and marble are repeated in the surface and reveals of the main reception desk. Fine design and finishes continue into the adjacent component area of offices and open work stations, uniting the entire space both visually and physically.

BMW Showroom and Service Pavilion   New York, New York

The design of this pavilion is analogous to the BMW product: Precise, technologically oriented and reflective of its essential functions. The form is simple and straightforward.

With strong, graphic, corporate identity guidelines firmly in place, BMW communicated specific design parameters. By absorbing the business and environments of BMW facilities all over the world, a trust was established which in turn allowed the risk of architectural innovation.

The plan combines showrooms and consumer contact areas with the mechanical functions of the shops by utilizing glass with varying degrees of translucency throughout the facility. Transparent glass exposes showroom, sales, and reception areas; Opaque glass in various shades of white and gray is used to shield repair, parking and storage areas from view.

A neutral palette of black, white, and gray is carried throughout the structure while product provides the only contrasting color. In the evening, the pavilion's six stories of glass stand out above low-rise industrial neighbors, luminous against the sky.

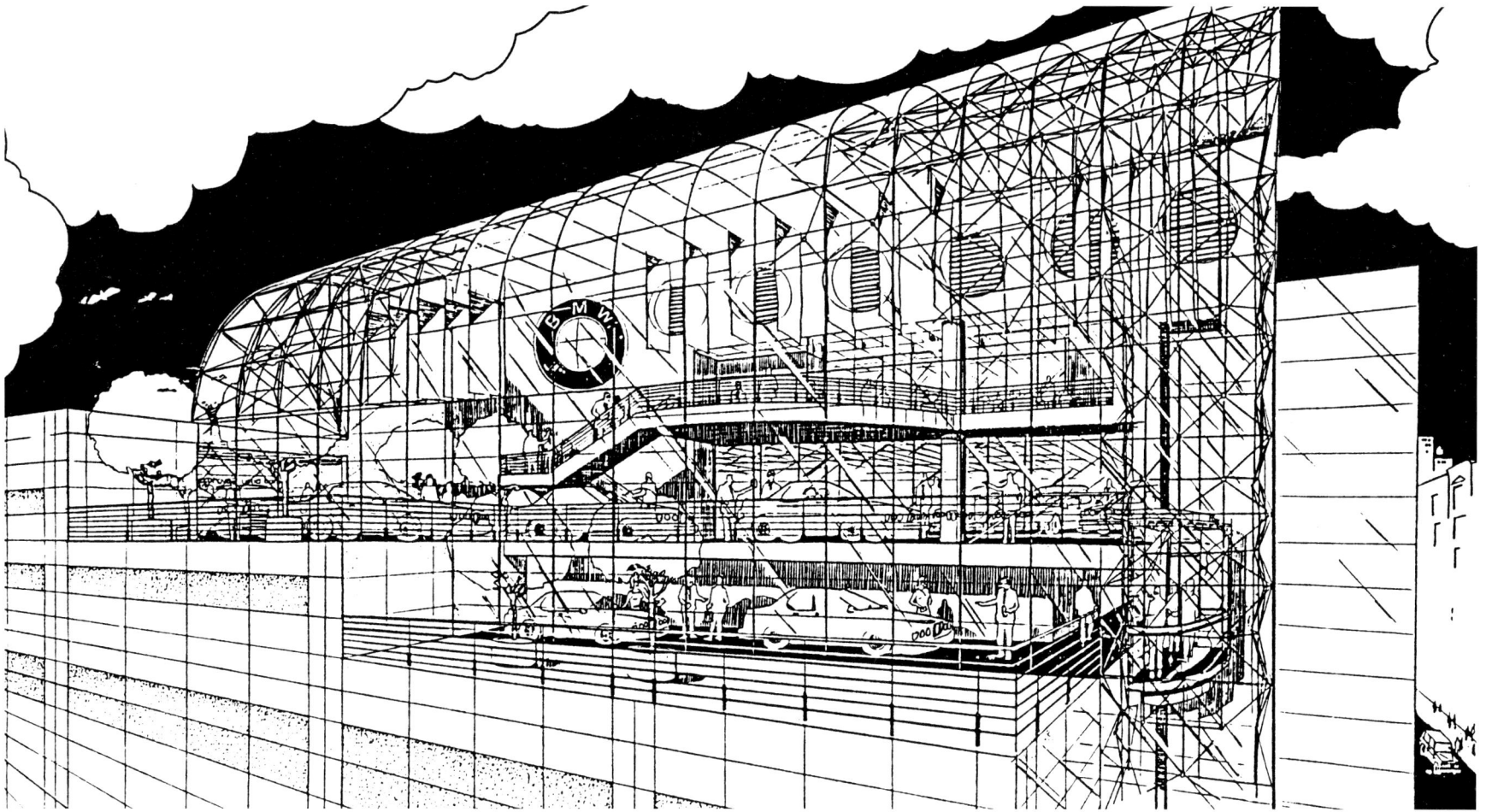

Sony Western Regional Operations Center San Jose, California

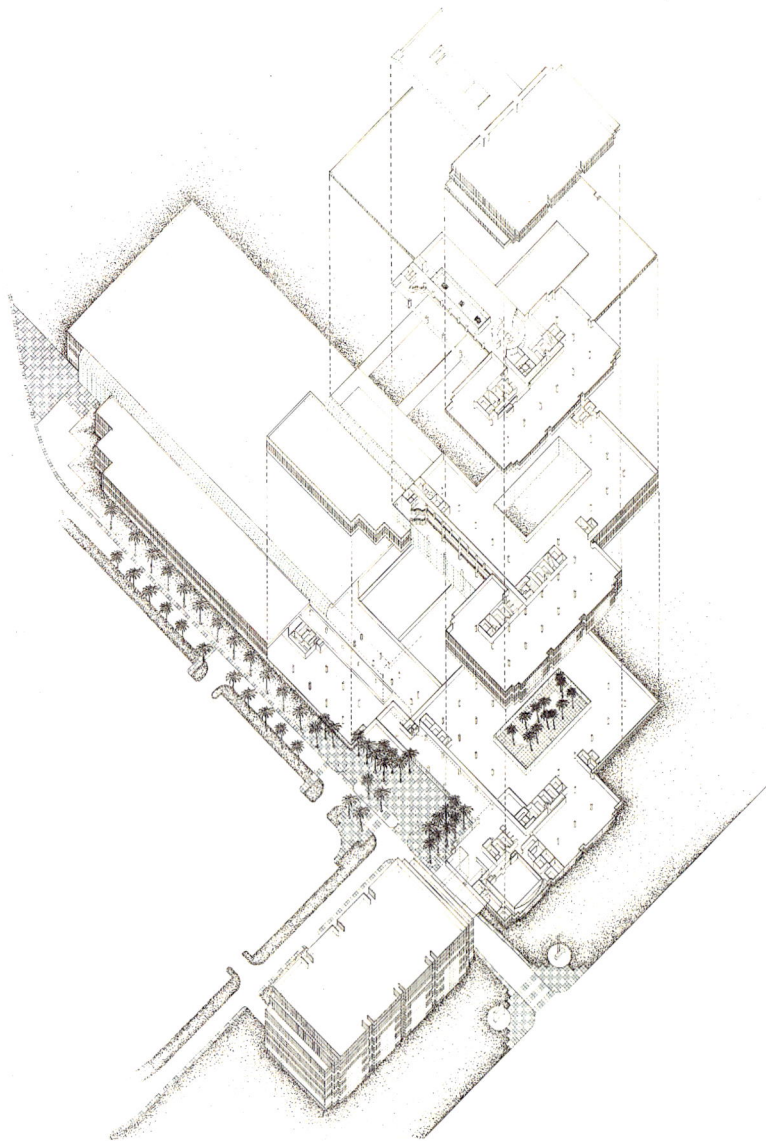

The Sony spirit and culture is the intense driving force behind Sony's product and staff. The northern California group formerly was composed of eight companies, located in three cities. This corporate fragmentation was a deterrent to staff interaction, communication, and the efficiency of the Sony team. The Spector Group was charged by Dr. Ron Sommer to create a Sony campus that would bring all regional companies to a single location: an environment that would meet today's program requirements, as well as projections for the years 1995, 1999, 2003, and beyond.

The facility is a resource base for management, distribution, technology, and research under one roof. Empowered within this building is one united Sony family sharing the facility, the technology, and the knowledge. This unity intensifies a high entrepreneurial spirit, stimulates motivation, and allows the Sony machine to perform at optimum levels. Multiple opportunities for employees and shared interactions, materials, and amenities reinforce a strong camaraderie.

The building design incorporates a philosophy of flexibility and modularity. Departmental zones of open office space, warehouse/distribution, research and development, and administrative support have been developed to maximize communication and efficiency. The entire facility maintains a 40-by-40-foot module, which allows for ease of reorganization of space and future expansion. Such flexibility also permits change or expansion with no interruption of day-to-day operations. Materials are simple, efficient, and of high quality, projecting Sony's character to staff, consumer, and the community.

Projecting to the community a sense of pride and a commitment to the environment, the building is raised on a platform of greenery. Parking, loading areas, and mechanical equipment are screened by the building itself, while offices look out to the mountain range beyond. Exposed technology will be purposeful as Sony's spirit is evident whether you drive through the main entry, enter the lobby, or walk through offices and research and development areas.

At the initial interview, Michael Spector took a risk and asked why we were hiding Sony's startling technology behind closed doors. I wondered the same thing.
— Ron Sommer, President, Sony Corporation of America

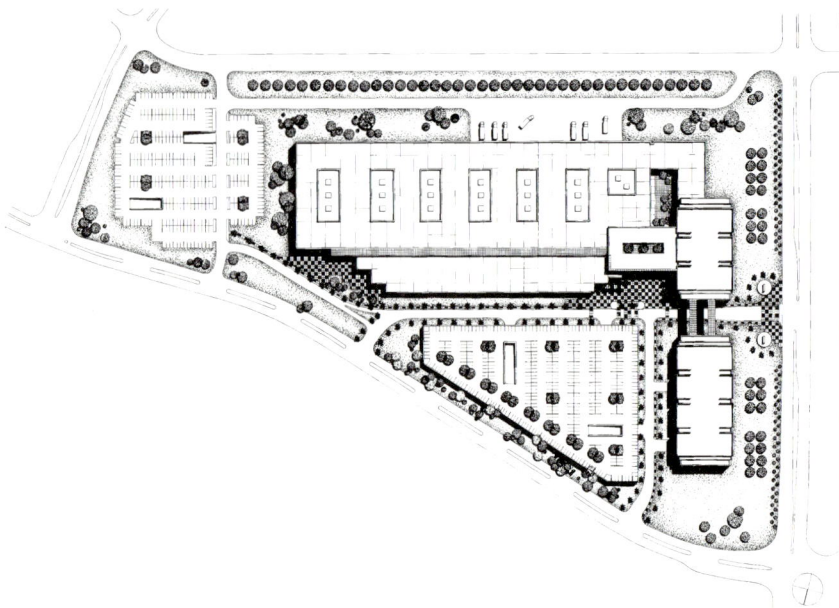

Cablevision Corporate Headquarters Huntington, New York

As improved communication technology draws the world closer together, corporate leaders are regrouping in response to internal quests for greater productivity and creativity. After growing from a single home base to fifteen locations across the northeast, Cablevision is now seeking to consolidate and unify their respective divisions.

The proposed headquarters will be sited in a wooded area, overlooking a state park. The plan calls for an abundance of trees and open plazas, with parking screened by landscaping and structure. Three stainless steel satellite dishes, rather like an honor guard, will stand proudly at the front of the building, incorporated into the architecture.

Upon entry, an atrium with multiple stairways and bridges links all four levels. This 450-foot linear space resembles a tree-lined streetscape, with studios, cafes, vertical circulation, and a specific retail outlet serving the corporation. On the upper levels, open work stations replace private offices, including the chairman's office which will look directly out on the atrium below. As the balconies step back, floor space gradually widens, creating greater lines of vision.

To foster communication, an open floor plan removes all barriers and allows employees greater access to each other. Typical corporate hierarchy is replaced by increased access for all staff. Informal meeting niches spread throughout the facility; arrangements of couches and chairs encourage casual conversation and the exchange of ideas.

I pay my monthly fee for cable
channels and now I have a
chance to break even.
– Michael Harris Spector

Nove Butovice Technology City   Prague, Czech Republic

The historic city of Prague has been hailed as the most industrialized and culturally sophisticated of the Eastern Bloc cities. Nove Butovice Technology City—located ten minutes from Prague—is being created to attract international business and to stimulate the economy. While early (post–World War II) master plans for this site were mainly for housing, new concepts include retail development, a trade center, public piazzas, and buildings interconnected with public walkways. Today, the Czech government seeks to create a central hub, a "Gateway to Prague."

The requirements of the town of Nove Butovice were studied, as were the needs of Prague. Since metros and roadways were already completed, the challenge was to create a cohesive community incorporating what was already in place. The buildings' design should express the future of technology. Metal and glass will expose the infrastructure and the energy within. Exterior moving sidewalks and pedestrian walkways will emphasize visibility. And since the charge of this city is to attract international business, amenities will abound.

The site chosen for the proposed Technology City project is just southwest of Prague and the River Moldau. One of four planned outer satellites, this project will comprise approximately one million square feet of office space and 150,000 square feet of retail space. A 600,000-square-foot trade center, a 500-room hotel, plus conference centers, banquet halls, and health club facilities are also planned.

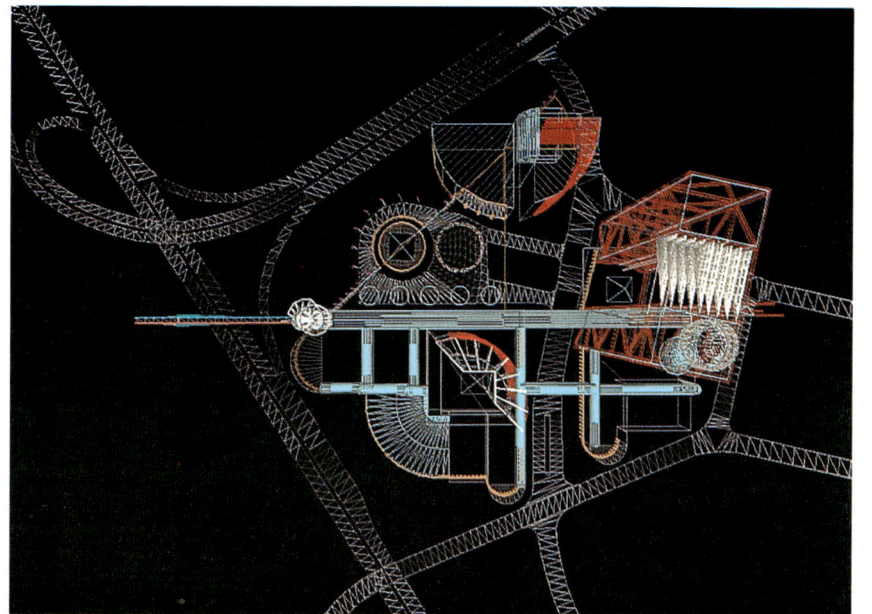

People's Republic of China

When working in a foreign country, it has been the practice of the Spector Group to form an alliance with a firm familiar with the land, language, and culture of that country. With local architects also involved, the Spector Group has formed an association with James Jao Architects of Manhattan to continue its development of work in the People's Republic of China.

Though vastly different from one another, the proposed structures on the following pages share a common concept. They are all vertical communities, designed for provinces of China hungry for services and technology. Each project will incorporate the latest in building intelligence, but will also maintain a sense of the Chinese culture in their relationship to function and open space.

All the projects will be mixed use, incorporating office, hotel/residential, retail, and recreational space. Together they will embrace the twenty-first century with architecture, technology, and services designed to attract the world traveler as well as local business groups.

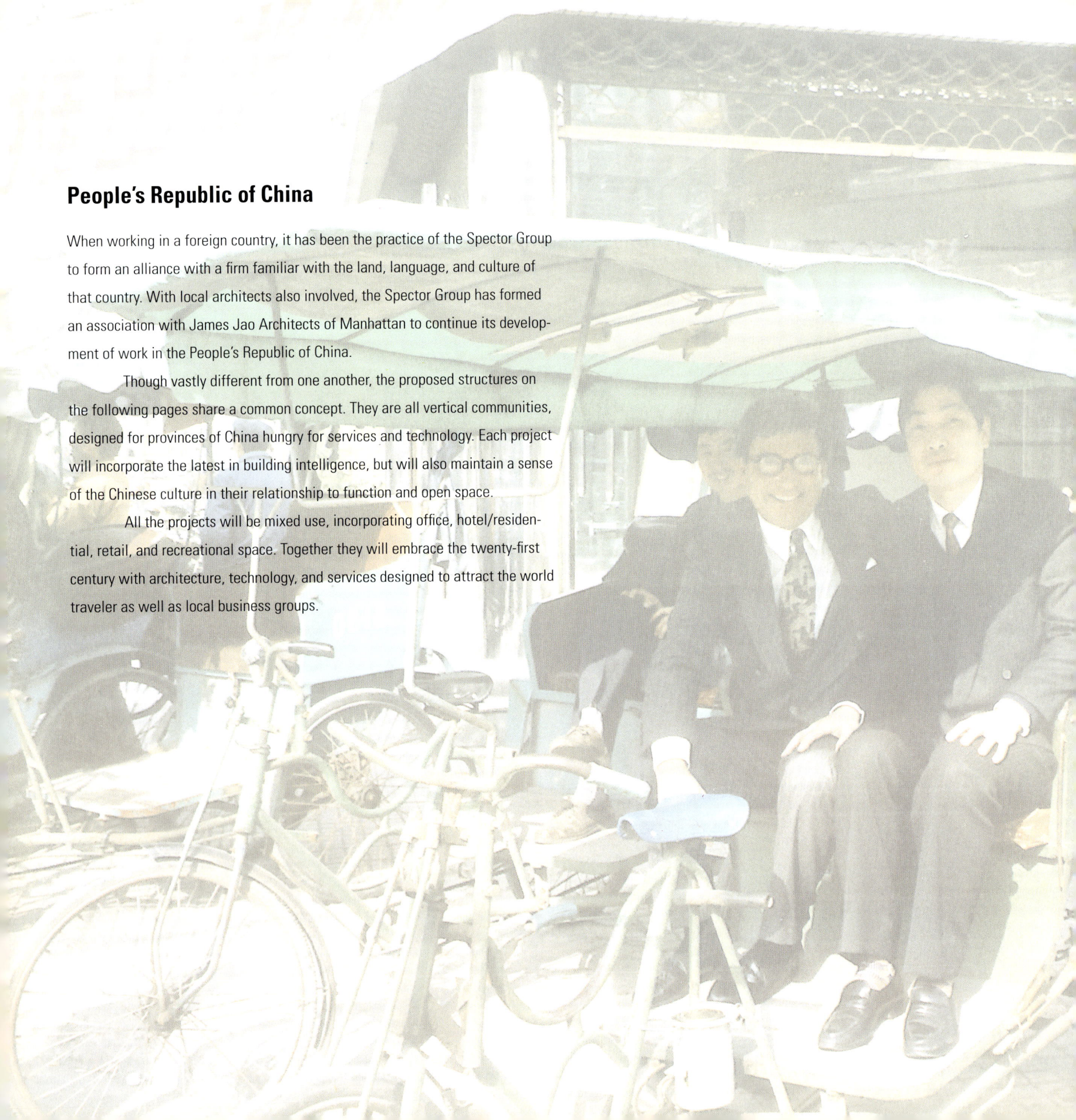

San Kei Commercial City Shenyang, China

A network of interdependent functions is united within this proposed complex, known as San Kei Commercial City. The structure will incorporate a covered retail arcade at its base and will be surmounted by individual residential and corporate office towers, the latter capped by a distinctive functional telecommunications crown.

The seven-story base respects the scale of its surroundings and invites pedestrian activity along one of Shenyang's high-density commercial thoroughfares. By placing the office lobby on the third level, retail space will be maximized below.

Rising above the covered retail arcade, a 35-story corporate office tower and 42-story residential tower will step back to create a distinctive skyline presence. Atop the office tower, a rooftop restaurant and observation deck are planned.

Fashion City Central   Dalian, China

This forty-story, mixed-use complex will present itself to Dalian with sculptural form and state-of-the-art technology. The three-story retail arcade, faced in stone, will create a bold base for a glass tower and will incorporate office, hotel, and banquet facilities.

A ground-level atrium will house an elegant lobby while a sky-level cutout in the facade will create a visually exciting, multilevel roof garden and open air dining area. The lower tower, spanning front to back, makes a striking, distinctive cap for this multi-use structure.

Jiu Hai Plaza Shanghai, China

A multiplicity of functions will be captured in the proposed Jiu Hai Plaza's 25-story mixed-use structure. These functions will include office and retail facilities, a 253-room luxury hotel, fitness center, conference center, banquet/exhibition hall, six restaurants, a main subway station, and mechanical, service, and support facilities required of a complex of this size and diversity.

The plaza's six-story retail arcade will be accentuated by a grand colonnade and a multistory windowed showroom. An adjacent, three-story triangular subway station will be enclosed with glass. This dynamic skylit element will guide pedestrians by escalator to the station and food court below, without intruding on other building functions.

The design plan calls for a main lobby rising above the four-story podium, and resting within a twenty-two-story skylit atrium space. Enclosed in spaceframe, the structure appears as a glass pavilion—with no visual means of structural support.

Jiu Hai Plaza's tower of spaceframe and glass will enclose two sightseeing elevators, which will yield unparalleled views of the city. At its end, the spaceframe structure will rise above and cap the building with a dramatically lit crown, visible from the entire peninsula.

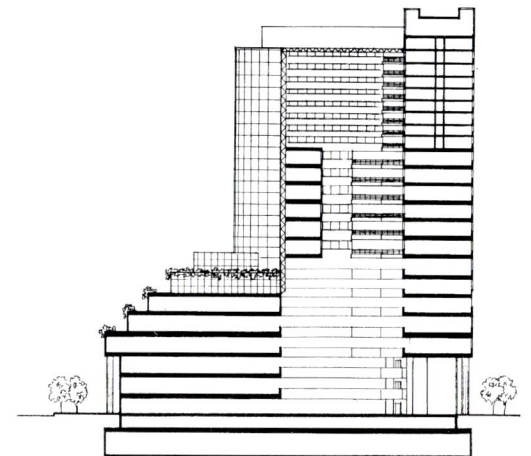

Zhong Hang Plaza   Shenzhen, China

With Shenzhen's vast need for infrastructure and services, Zhong Hang Plaza is projected to be a community unto itself. Public spaces will be interspersed throughout this mixed-use center while 24-hour services will reflect an interior metropolis. As a result, newly developed urban planning concepts will be utilized to optimize accessibility and egress.

Upon entry, a vertical and horizontal "Main Street" with offshoot avenues to services culminate in a huge public space on the ground level. This expanse incorporates an indoor ice rink, dining, entertainment, and recreational amenities. Avenues off this 27-story skylit atrium galleria lead to a 72-story office tower, 16-story residential/hotel, 8-story retail arcade, and four levels of underground parking with space for 800 automobiles and 5,600 bicycles. A full-loading terminal, unique to the city, services the building's diverse facilities, which include a food court, restaurants and tea houses, department store and retail shops, amusement park, theatre, museum, art galleries, private conference facilities, library, and multiple fitness and recreational facilities including racquetball courts, locker rooms, and extensive spaces for the practice of martial arts.

The 72-story cylindrical tower rises to its full height with the north elevation revealing a carved slice infilled with terraces that emphasize its verticality. The west elevation of the tower is rectangular in shape, embraced on both ends by the curved arms of the circular tower. The fenestration is square and slightly recessed in contrast with the continuous banded glass of the curved facade. A series of three-story lobbies serve as breakout spaces with elevator access to fulfill the requirements of Chinese building codes, which demand emergency egress or breakout areas every fifteen stories. The crown of the tower is a three-story, glass-enclosed restaurant catering to the cuisine of China's varied provinces.

The northern facade, a more structured simplified geometry, faces the Old City in respect to its architectural roots. The southern facade is curvilinear, facing the South China Sea with an eye to the city's future aspirations. Green-tinted glass exposes the building's structure while white glass emphasizes the curve and accentuates the pristine profile desired.

Though "twenty-first century" in technology, Zhong Hang Plaza pays tribute to the Chinese culture with its extensive access and availability of skylit indoor areas and outdoor spaces. Rooftop gardens and outdoor terraces at punctuated levels of the structure respect its users' desire for spaces for meditation and relaxation while enjoying the comforts and technology of the Western world.

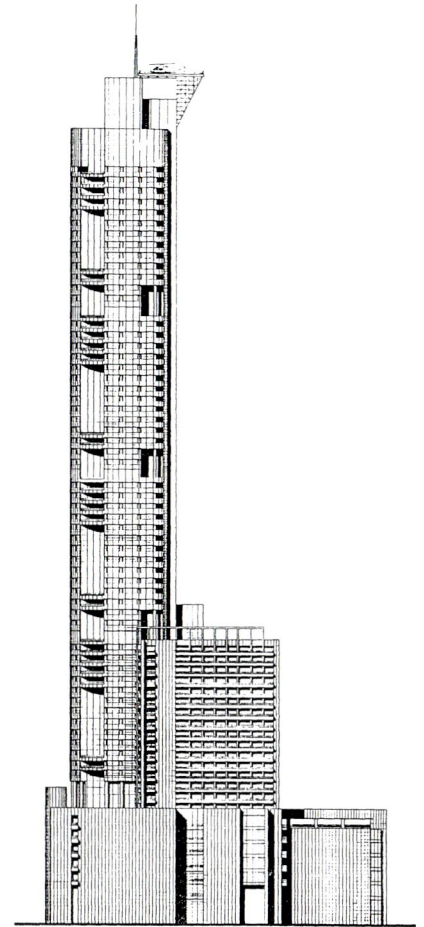

Federal Building and United States Courthouse   Islip, New York

Rarely, does an architectural firm have the opportunity to design the nations largest Federal Building and United States Courthouse for the General Services Administration. The Spector Group and Richard Meier and Partners have embarked on a collaboration to meet this challenging commission. The 850,000-square-foot program defines twenty-one new courtrooms to accommodate the current needs of the U.S. Courts of the Eastern District of New York. Offices for the executive branch agencies of the U.S. Attorney, FBI, IRS, OSHA, and the DEA are also included in the program.

The building is an eleven-story bar configuration, with two wings separated by its core and a full-height atrium. Because of the unusual floor-to-floor heights required for the courtrooms, this is equivalent to a sixteen-story office building. The building's east wing houses the District Courts and related facilities. The west wing houses the Bankruptcy Courts. Two volumes have been added to either side of the bar configuration: a three-story Ceremonial Court and a training/conference facility on the ground floor. A nine-story volume on the south side houses the entrance lobby, security, and public waiting areas. Three independent circulation systems, public/staff, judicial and prisoner, insure privacy and security.

On the south elevation, a large entry rotunda in the form of an inverted cone extends nearly the full height of the building. Skylit at the roof and sheathed in aluminum panels, the rotunda is connected to the main building by walkways at each court floor level.

When Richard Meier and I strategized our chances of being selected, Richard stated, "I've won all over Europe, but I'm a black sheep in America." I replied, "This is our first government submission." We gave it our all, night and day…we were selected.
– Michael Harris Spector

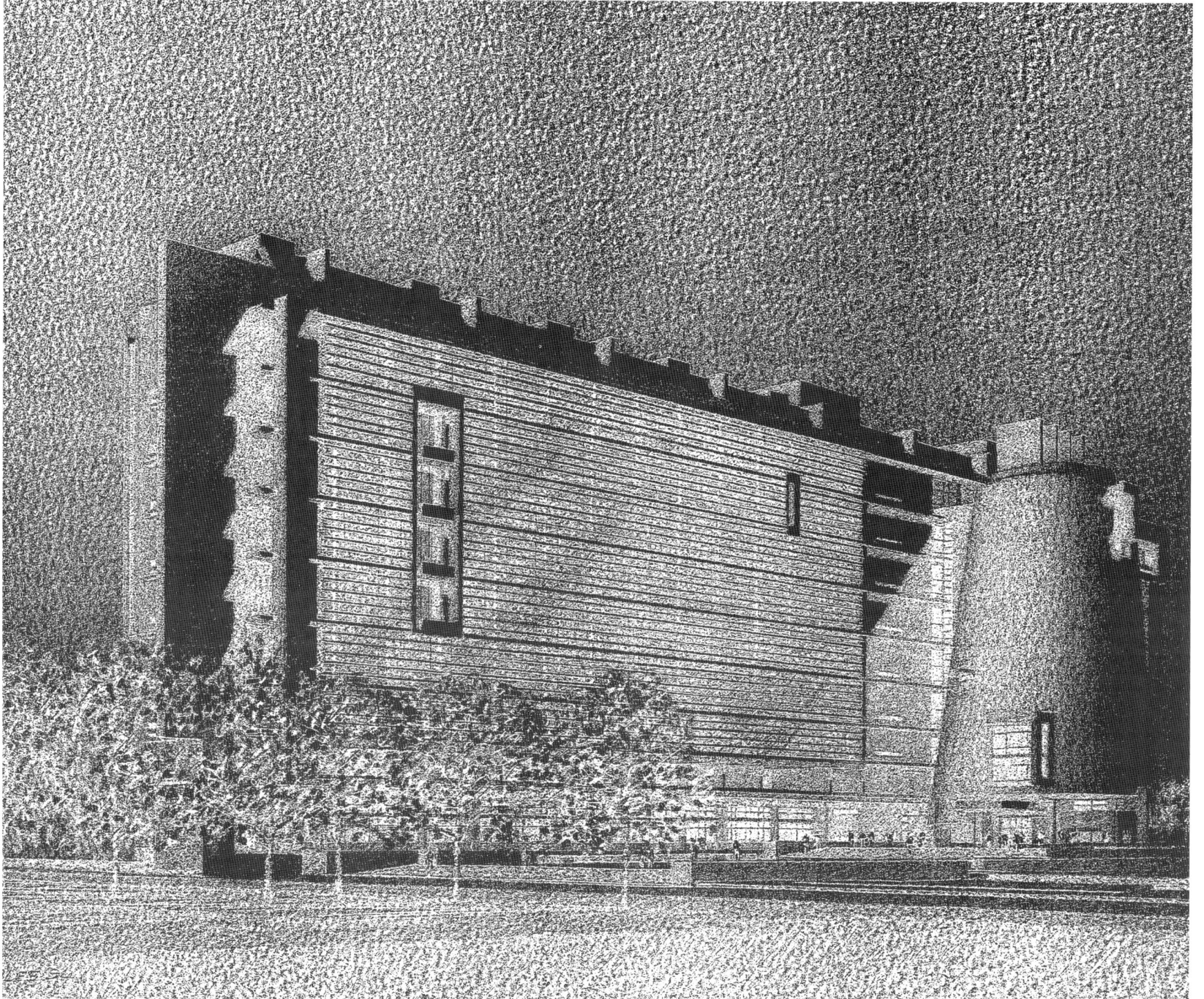

Meadowlands Town Center   Bergen County, New Jersey

A new city in progress, planned by the Spector Group, propels the New York Metropolitan Area into the next century. On a 600-acre site bordering the New Jersey Turnpike and the Meadowlands Sports Complex, the largest planned community in the region's history will evolve from what is now nonproductive marshland.

Meadowlands Town Center will consist of corporate office buildings; 6,200 housing units; regional and neighborhood retail stores; hotels, cultural, entertainment, and recreational facilities; and a mass transit center. In addition, approximately one-half of the site will be transformed into ecologically valued wetlands, teeming with plant and wildlife.

The focus of the entire development is the "Main Street" concept featuring the Meadowlands Town Center. This public space will incorporate a major sculpture, fountain, reflecting pool/ice rink, amphitheater, and a circular hotel framed over Main Street. Included in this component is a large scale pavilion surrounded by water and a landscaped court. It is anticipated that this pavilion will accommodate cultural, entertainment, and educational-based programs. This vibrant urban center will be alive with activity day and night.

Afterword   Partnership is chemistry, the bond created between people to move the process forward.

When I decided to join my father and brother Scott at the Spector Group five years ago, I knew that to achieve the highest degree of design excellence, a working chemistry among the three of us had to be present. I had the base. I have been surrounded by people whose love for the field far surpasses any other physical emotion. While growing up, my father and grandfather, Charles, used to take me to see their buildings and they would educate me in the process of architecture. Entering college, I was fortunate enough to have a design professor who shared the same passion for the field as I. Dr. James Chaffers, at The University of Michigan College of Architecture, instilled in me his basic, fundamental principles of good design. I refer to his teachings to this day.

For me, architecture has always been a central cultural institution valued above all for its provisions of equilibrium. These qualities arise from the geometric purity of its formal composition.

Every work of architecture represents an attempt to transcend mere shelter and accommodation. Building is specific, the literal translation of a program into bricks and mortar. Architecture is general, raising building to a poetic level by embracing the cultural continuum: form, style and expression. They are the otherness that lends building the resonance of art. It is what encompasses "otherness" that creates atypical architecture.

"Atypical" is pushing the modern esthetic just a bit further than the masters of modernism took it, forcing it to a bursting point and then stopping just before the break comes. The intricacy of our design approach is an exercise in taunting chaos, such that we do not actually feel the chaos at all, but instead feel so much a sense of control that the result is almost serene.

I believe that a Spector building is a Spector building, recognizable not by mere tangible icons, but by the essence of it, the articulations of the intangibles.

Collaborators

Mark Abramson
Stacey Ackley
Frank Adamowicz
Vincent Affenita
Tunc Aksoy
Paul Anderson
Maria Anza
Nina Anza
Alice Ascetta
Kathleen Avino
Harold Bade
Bob Barbal
Jay Baron
Gloria Barsky
Douglas Bartolomeo
Greg Basmajian
Rosemary Basmajian
Linda Bauer
Sara Baume
Eileen Beatty
Steve Bello
Robert Bierman
Thomas Bitnar
Victoria Blau
Lawrence Brauerman
Kathi Burns
Edward Butt
Nick Caivano
Chip Calcagni
Greg Campofranco
Neil Cappana
Dominic Cardone
Kathleen Carey
Ianthe Carpen
George Chin
Shari Cohen
Catherine Cotumaccio
David Crawford
Raymond Cristobal
Charles Croigny
Sean Cuddahy
Lynn Cusimano
Jaye Czyzyk
Charles D'Alessio
Bill Davis

Sam Davis
Richard DeMarco
Louise DePrimo
Madeline Diano
Rick DiFilippi
Matt DiGiamio
Anthony DiGuiseppe
Andy DiLauro
Roger Diller
Mike diPiero
Anthony Donatich
Sylvia Donnelly
Dick Eaton
Peter Elkin
Michael Farrell
Danielle Felsen
Mitch Fier
Debbie Finkelstein
John Fondrissi
Tom Fraehmke
Vincent Franchi
Edward Friedman
Jeff Friedman
Christine Friello
Susan Gaskin
Suzanne Geiss
Terry Geller
Arthur Gentile
Jane Felsen Gertler
John Giaccio
Maureen Going
Charles Golub
Jan Gould
Joanne Graves
John Gregorio
Kathy Grillo
Richard Grunseich
Kathleen Haas
Alex Hadaro
Dov Hadas
Albert Han
Joe Handler
Sat Harish
Nancy Hart
Regina Hartigan

Scott Hayden
Phillip Heller
Paul Heretakis
Michael Hirschkorn
Richard Hong
Milan Hospodka
Kathleen Hynes
Arthur Johnson
Patricia Kettle
Pamela Wright Knakal
Marcelo Kohan
Richard Kornblath
John Kraft
Roma Kucaj
George Kuchek
Gary Lawrance
Irene Lennon
Joan Liebman
Karen Lindie
Alicia Lindner
Paul Llopis
Charles Lobell
Donna Long
Donna Macchia
Erwin Machol
John Machovec
Maria Mainolfi
Patricia Manfre
Michael J. Mannetta
Joann Mannino
Rosemarie Margino
Christine Martel
Jim Martino
Frank Martucci
Gregg Matchton
Arthur McDonald
Ronald J. McDonald
Michael McNerney
William Medlow
Frank Messano
Scott Miller
Khalid Mohammed
Thomas Mojo
John Monti
Peter Moore

Thomas Moran
Jim Morel
Frank Mrakovcic
Nancy Mrowka
Fay Munson
Lisa Orlando
Donald Oster
Danita Otruba
Ralph Ottaiano
Lori Ottavio
Richard Paroly
John Patey
Gerri Pelliccie
Thomas Penn
Leda Pierce
Ci Hang Ping
Thomas Pirkl
Michael Pitman
Paul Ponce
Zhang You Quan
Kelly Quinn
James Ramenthol
Joseph Randazzo
Renee Reichert
John Reilly
Joseph Reilly
Jerry Rein
Milton Reiner
Ron Reisen
Johnathan Reo
Louis Reyes
Pia Rosario
Irving Roth
David Rozzi
Gary Ruderman
Michael Ruegammer
Janet Ruggiero
Jeanette Sabino
Patricia Schachter
Ethel Schaffer
David Schefer
William Scherer
Edna Guilor Segal
John Seifert
Mindy Seldon

Mercedes Sempliner
Eric Singer
Irwin Sirota
Charles Skronski
Bob Smith
Jeff Spanier
Charles Spector
Joan Spector
Jolie Spector
Marc Spector
Michael Harris Spector
Scott Spector
Mark Squeo
Christine Stanzione
Marjorie Stave
Stanley Stevens
Doreen Stewart
Mark Stumer
Peter K. Toh
Gerard Torchio
Stacy Travell
Steven Umansky
Tara Valone
Kevin Van Hulse
Harry Van Meter
Christine Vassalo
Robert Verbanac
Ben Videna
Thomas Virzi
Peter Vonderleith
Donna Walczuk
Renate Walker
Pauline Waney
Kenneth Wattenberg
Dick Wey
Christopher Wey
Charles White
Christopher White
Paul Wolfthal
Scott Woolsey
Kin Yan Yan
Irene Yu
Lu Zheng Zhong
Patricia Zinon

Representative Project Portfolio

Project Grace Building
Location Great Neck, New York
Dates 1968/70
Project Team *Michael Harris Spector*, Alex Hadaro,
Charles Skronski

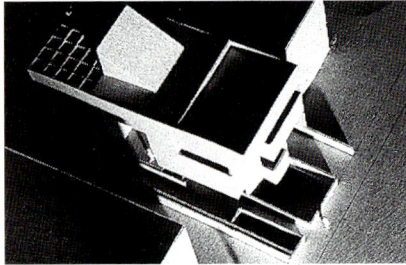

Project Rich Residence
Location Tel Aviv, Israel
Dates 1967/69
Designer Michael Harris Spector

Project Michael H. Spector Studios
Location Great Neck, New York
Dates 1968/69
Project Team *Michael Harris Spector*, Alex Hadaro,
Charles Lobell, Dominic Cardone,
Richard Wey

Project Mah Jong Restaurant
Location Syosset, New York
Dates 1967/68
Designer Michael Harris Spector

Project Manufacturers Hanover Trust
Location Woodbury, New York
Dates 1968/70
Project Team *Michael Harris Spector*, Charles Lobell,
Alex Hadaro, Richard Wey, Eric Singer

Project Executive Plaza
Location Great Neck, New York
Dates 1968/70
Designer Michael Harris Spector

Project Jaromor Corporation
Location Great Neck, New York
Dates 1969/71
Project Team *Michael Harris Spector*,
Dominic Cardone

Project Expressway Center
Location Roslyn, New York
Dates 1968/70
Project Team *Michael Harris Spector*, Alex Hadaro,
Charles Lobell, Charles Skronski,
Mark Stumer

Project Hempstead Plaza
Location Hempstead, New York
Dates 1969/72
Project Team *Michael Harris Spector*, Alex Hadaro,
John Monti, Richard Wey, Harry Van
Meter, Jeff Spanier, Charles Skronski

Project Hellinger Residence
Location Greenwich, Connecticut
Dates 1968/69
Project Team *Michael Harris Spector*, Harold Bade,
Richard Wey

Project Estates Residential Center
Location Great Neck, New York
Dates 1969/70
Project Team *Michael Harris Spector*, Jeff Spanier,
Richard Wey, Harold Bade

Project Squire Restaurant
Location Great Neck, New York
Date 1969
Project Team *Michael Harris Spector*, Eric Singer

Project Allstate Headquarters
Location Farmingville, New York
Dates 1970/74
Project Team *Michael Harris Spector*, Dominic Cardone, Thomas Mojo, Ronald McDonald, John Monti, Robert Barbal, Anthony DiLauro

Project Pan Am Health Spa
Location Manhasset, New York
Dates 1970/71
Designer Michael Harris Spector

Project Tam O'Shanter Golf Club
Location Brookville, New York
Dates 1971/73
Project Team *Michael Harris Spector*, Ronald McDonald, Thomas Mojo, Mark Stumer, John Monti

Project Park Properties
Location Melville, New York
Dates 1970/72
Designer Michael Harris Spector

Project SunHarbor Health Related Facility
Location Roslyn, New York
Dates 1972/74
Project Team *Michael Harris Spector*, Anthony DiLauro, Robert Barbal, Thomas Mojo, Harry Van Meter

Project Temple Beth Sholom
Location Lawrence, New York
Dates 1970/71
Project Team *Michael Harris Spector*, Scott Miller, Robert Barbal, John Monti

Project Spector Residence
Location Westhampton, New York
Dates 1972/74
Designer Michael Harris Spector

Project Residential Complex
Location Ecuador, South America
Dates 1971/73
Project Team *Michael Harris Spector*, David Crawford, Nancy Mrowka, Ronald McDonald

Project Great Neck Youth Theatre
Location Great Neck, New York
Dates 1972/73
Project Team *Michael Harris Spector*, Scott Woolsey

Project The Institute for Community Health Long Island Jewish Hospital
Location New Hyde Park, New York
Date 1971
Designer Michael Harris Spector

Project Extebank
Location Hauppauge, New York
Dates 1972/74
Project Team *Michael Harris Spector*, Thomas Mojo, Scott Woolsey

Project Residential Complex
Location Glen Cove, New York
Dates 1972/74
Designer Michael Harris Spector

Project The McBurney School
Location New York, New York
Dates 1977/78
Project Team *Michael Harris Spector,* Ronald McDonald, Thomas Mojo

Project Crossways Center
Location Woodbury, New York
Dates 1974/76
Project Team *Michael Harris Spector,* Charles Lobell, John Monti, Robert Barbal, Scott Miller

Project Colonial Building
Location Great Neck, New York
Date 1977
Designer Michael Harris Spector

Project Drew Chemical Headquarters
Location Boonton, New Jersey
Dates 1975/77
Project Team *Michael Harris Spector,* Thomas Mojo, Dominic Cardone, Mark Stumer, John Monti, Robert Barbal, Anthony DiLauro

Project Jericho Plaza II
Location Jericho, New York
Dates 1977/79
Project Team *Michael Harris Spector,* John Monti, Robert Barbal, Anthony DiLauro, Dominic Cardone

Project IBM•Jericho Plaza
Location Jericho, New York
Dates 1976/78
Project Team *Michael Harris Spector,* Thomas Mojo, Dominic Cardone, Robert Barbal

Project United Technologies
Location Westport, Connecticut
Dates 1977/79
Project Team *Michael Harris Spector,* Scott Woolsey, Robert Barbal, Richard Wey, Kenneth Wattenberg

Project Bikoff Center
Location College Point, New York
Dates 1976/78
Project Team *Michael Harris Spector,* Thomas Mojo, Kathleen Avino, Dominic Cardone

Project Dime Savings Bank
Location Port Washington, New York
Dates 1977
Project Team *Michael Harris Spector,* Scott Woolsey, Robert Barbal, John Patey, Anthony Donatich

Project Hilton Hotel
Location Danbury, Connecticut
Dates 1977/79
Project Team *Michael Harris Spector,* Thomas Mojo, Dominic Cardone

Project Prudential Insurance Company
Location Huntington, New York
Dates 1977/79
Project Team *Michael Harris Spector,* Dominic Cardone, Thomas Mojo, Mark Stumer, Robert Barbal, John Monti, Kenneth Wattenberg

Project Saks Fifth Avenue
Location New York, New York
Dates 1977/78
Project Team *Michael Harris Spector*, Mark Stumer

Project IBM Global Communications Center
Location White Plains, New York
Dates 1978/81
Project Team *Peter K. Toh*, Robert Barbal, Jan Gould, Dominic Cardone, Kenneth Wattenberg, John Seifert

Project Rodi Corporation
Location Roslyn, New York
Dates 1978/79
Project Team *Michael Harris Spector*, Mark Stumer, John Monti, Robert Barbal, Kenneth Wattenberg

Project Hilton Hotel
Location Melville, New York
Dates 1978/80
Project Team *Michael Harris Spector*, William Medlow

Project Parsippany Complex
Location Parsippany, New York
Date 1978
Designer Michael Harris Spector

Project Bienenfeld Industries
Location Port Washington, New York
Dates 1978/80
Project Team *Michael Harris Spector*, Thomas Mojo, John Monti, Robert Barbal

Project Morristown Center
Location Morristown, New Jersey
Dates 1978/80
Designer Michael Harris Spector

Project Automatic Data Processing
Location Melville, New York
Dates 1978/81
Project Team *Michael Harris Spector*, Robert Barbal, Kenneth Wattenberg, John Monti

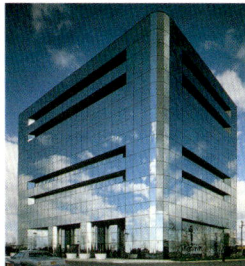

Project 666 Old Country Road
Location Garden City, New York
Dates 1978/80
Project Team *Michael Harris Spector*, Mark Stumer, Steve Bello, Dominic Cardone, Robert Barbal, Jan Gould

Project Schulman/Divney
Location White Plains, New York
Dates 1978/80
Project Team *Michael Harris Spector*, John Monti, Dominic Cardone

Project Avant Garde Optics
Location Port Washington, New York
Dates 1978/80
Project Team *Michael Harris Spector, Thomas Mojo*, John Patey

Project Livingston Mall
Location Livingston, New Jersey
Dates 1978/80
Project Team *Michael Harris Spector*, Dominic Cardone, David Crawford, Raymond Cristobal

Project 3333 New Hyde Park Road
Location North Hills, New York
Dates 1979/81
Project Team *Michael Harris Spector*, Thomas Mojo, John Monti, Robert Barbal

Project 40 Cuttermill Road
Location Great Neck, New York
Dates 1979/80
Project Team *Michael Harris Spector*, John Patey, Edna Guilor, John Seifert, Michael Mannetta

Project IBM
Location Rye, New York
Dates 1979/81
Project Team *Michael Harris Spector*, Kenneth Wattenberg, Mark Stumer, John Monti, Michael Mannetta, John Seifert

Project International Apparel Mart
Location New York, New York
Dates 1980/81
Designer Michael Harris Spector

Project Manufacturers Hanover Trust
Location Hicksville, New York
Dates 1979/81
Project Team *Michael Harris Spector*, Jan Gould, Anthony DiLauro, Douglas Bartolomeo, Michael Mannetta, Dominic Cardone, Richard Paroly

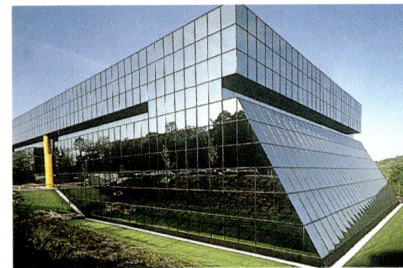

Project IBM Research Center
Location Mt. Pleasant, New York
Dates 1980/82
Project Team *Michael J. Mannetta*, Kenneth Wattenberg, Anthony DiLauro, Terry Geller, John Siefert, John Monti

Project Exxon Chemical
Location Darien, Connecticut
Dates 1979/81
Project Team *Michael Harris Spector*, Thomas Mojo, Dominic Cardone

Project Northtown Retail Center
Location Manhasset, New York
Dates 1980/83
Project Team *Peter K. Toh*, Gerard Torchio, Arthur Gentile, John Monti, John Machovec, Ianthe Carpen, Roger Diller

Project Stackler/Gold Center
Location Rockville Center, New York
Dates 1979/81
Project Team *Michael Harris Spector*, Anthony DiLauro, John Patey

Project New York Hilton
Location New York, New York
Dates 1980/83
Project Team *Peter K. Toh*, Dominic Cardone, Greg Basmajian, Anthony Donatich

Project EAB World Headquarters
Location Uniondale, New York
Dates 1979/83
Project Team *Michael Harris Spector*, Ralph Ottaiano, John Fondrissi, John Monti, James Martino, Jan Gould, Michael Mannetta, Charles Golub, Paul Ponce, Richard Grunseich, Anthony DiLauro, Dominic Cardone, Vincent Franchi, Michael Ruegammer, Michael diPiero, Edna Guilor

Project Hartsdale Residential Community
Location Hartsdale, New York
Dates 1980/83
Project Team *Michael Harris Spector*, Ralph Ottaiano, Michael McNerney

Project International Business Center
Location White Plains, New York
Dates 1980/83
Project Team *Michael J. Mannetta*, Charles Golub, Art Gentile, John Monti, Joseph Randazzo, William Medlow, Richard DeMarco

Project Hilton Hotel
Location Somerset, New Jersey
Dates 1980/83
Project Team *Jan Gould*, John Monti, John Seifert, William Medlow

Project Cablevision Headquarters
Location Woodbury, New York
Dates 1980/82
Project Team *Peter K. Toh, Jan Gould*, Dominic Cardone, Frank Adamowicz, Tom Moran, Ed Friedman

Project Atrium Corporate Complex
Location Somerset, New Jersey
Date 1980
Project Team *Michael Harris Spector, Michael J. Mannetta*, John Monti, Jeff Friedman, William Scherer, John Seifert, Vincent Franchi, Richard Grunseich, Jan Gould, Edna Guilor, Douglas Bartolomeo, Anthony Donatich

Project CMP Publications
Location Great Neck, New York
Dates 1980/83
Project Team *Michael Harris Spector*, John Monti, Dominic Cardone, John Patey, Doug Bartolomeo

Project AT&T
Location Somerset, New Jersey
Dates 1981/83
Project Team *Michael J. Mannetta, Jan Gould*, Charles Golub, Anthony DiLauro, John Seifert, Richard Grunseich

Project Grumman Data Systems
Location Woodbury, New York
Dates 1980/83
Project Team *Thomas Mojo*, Scott Woolsey, Jeff Friedman, Peter Toh

Project Spector Group Studios
Location North Hills, New York
Dates 1981/83
Project Team *Michael Harris Spector*, Gary Ruderman, Anthony DiLauro, Richard Grunseich, Edward Butt, William Scherer, Ralph Ottaiano

Project Route 110 Complex
Location Huntington, New York
Dates 1980/82
Project Team *Michael J. Mannetta*, Richard DeMarco, Roger Diller, Jeff Friedman, Michael McNerney

Project Grumman Corporation
Location Woodbury, New York
Dates 1981/83
Project Team *Michael Harris Spector*, Kenneth Wattenberg, John Monti

Project IBM Marketing Prototype
Location Jericho, New York
Dates 1980/82
Project Team *Michael Harris Spector*, Ralph Ottaiano, Edna Guilor, Michael Mannetta

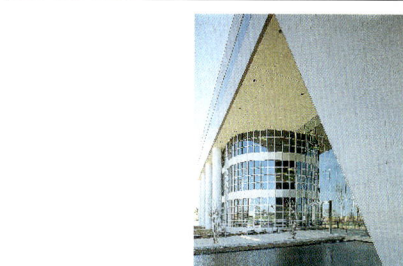

Project Merrill Lynch
Location Somerset, New Jersey
Dates 1981/83
Project Team *Michael J. Mannetta*, Robert Barbal, Anthony DiLauro, Douglas Bartolomeo, Edna Guilor, Anthony Donatich, John Monti

Project Extebank Interiors
Location New York, New York
Date 1982
Project Team *Peter K. Toh, Michael Ruegammer*, Jan Gould, Gregory Campofranco

Project Somerset Cali Center
Location Somerset, New Jersey
Date 1983
Project Team *Michael J. Mannetta*, Edna Guilor, Gregory Basmajian, Roger Diller, John Reilly

Project Merrill Lynch
Location Somerset, New Jersey
Dates 1982/84
Project Team *Michael J. Mannetta*, Robert Barbal, Anthony DiLauro

Project Merrill Lynch
Location Somerset, New Jersey
Dates 1983/86
Project Team *Michael Harris Spector, Michael J. Mannetta*, William Scherer, Joseph Reilly

Project United States Postal Service
Location Huntington, New York
Dates 1982/86
Project Team *Peter K. Toh*, Kenneth Wattenberg, Scott Woolsey, Anthony DiLauro, Vincent Franchi

Project Towson Center
Location Towson, Maryland
Dates 1983/85
Project Team *Peter K. Toh*, Dominic Cardone, Ralph Ottaiano

Project Chase Manhattan Bank
Location Mitchell Field, New York
Dates 1982/83
Project Team *Peter K. Toh*, John Gregorio, Gregory Basmajian, Thomas Bitnar, Vincent Franchi, Jay Baron

Project Citicorp Center
Location Shrewsbury, New Jersey
Date 1983
Project Team *Michael J. Mannetta*, Ralph Ottaiano, Jay Baron

Project Merck & Company
Location Somerset, New Jersey
Dates 1982/85
Project Team *Michael J. Mannetta*, Edna Guilor

Project
Location
Date
Designer

Project Piscataway Corporate Center
Location Piscataway, New Jersey
Date 1983
Project Team *Peter K. Toh*, Kenneth Wattenberg, William Scherer, John Seifert, Patricia Schachter

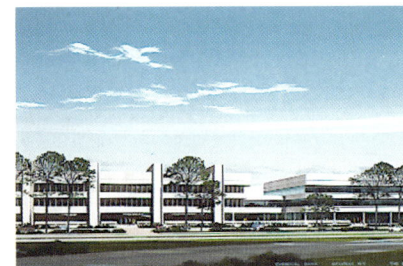

Project Expressway Complex
Location Long Island, New York
Date 1983
Project Team Michael Harris Spector

Project NYNEX
Location White Plains, New York
Dates 1983/85
Project Team *Michael Harris Spector, Peter K. Toh,* Kenneth Wattenberg, Paul Ponce, Douglas Bartolomeo, Richard Grunseich, John Patey

Project Grumman Data Systems
Location Suffolk, New York
Dates 1983/85
Project Team *Peter K. Toh,* John Seifert, William Scherer, Frank Messano, Edward Butt, Scott Woolsey, William Medlow, Vincent Franchi

Project Cerro Wire and Cable
Location Syosset, New York
Date 1983
Project Team *Michael J. Mannetta,* Paul Heretakis

Project Municipal Savings and Loan
Location Towson, Maryland
Date 1983
Project Team *Michael Harris Spector, Peter K. Toh,* Kenneth Wattenberg, John Giaccio, John Gregorio

Project Mount Laurel Building #1
Location Mount Laurel, New Jersey
Dates 1983/84
Project Team *Michael J. Mannetta,* David Crawford, John Patey, Paul Ponce

Project Long Island Savings Bank
Location Huntington, New York
Dates 1984/87
Project Team *Peter K. Toh,* Frank Messano, William Medlow, George Kuchek, Richard Grunseich, Dov Hadas, Gerard Torchio, Maria Anza, John Kraft

Project Roslyn Highlands Firehouse
Location Roslyn, New York
Dates 1984/85
Project Team *Peter K. Toh,* Frank Messano, Charles D'Alessio, Roger Diller, John Kraft, John Patey, Joseph Reilly

Project 777 Northern Boulevard
Location Manhasset, New York
Date 1984
Project Team *Peter K. Toh,* Roger Diller, John Patey

Project 60 Cuttermill Road
Location Great Neck, New York
Dates 1984/86
Project Team *Michael Harris Spector,* Dominic Cardone, Rick DiFilippi

Project Horizon Center
Location Hollywood, Florida
Dates 1984/86
Project Team *Peter K. Toh,* John Patey, John Seifert, Frank Messano, Vincent Franchi

Project United States Tennis Association
Location New York, New York
Dates 1984/85
Project Team *Michael Harris Spector,* Gregory Campofranco, Pamela Wright Knakal, Vincent Franchi, Paul Llopis, Frank Messano, Terry Geller

Project Plaza 100 Condominiums
Location Great Neck, New York
Dates 1984/86
Project Team *Michael Harris Spector,* Peter Toh, Edward Butt, John Giaccio, Gregory Campofranco

Project Commerce Bank
Location Mount Laurel, New Jersey
Dates 1984/85
Project Team *Michael J. Mannetta,* David Crawford

Project 80 Cuttermill Road
Location Great Neck, New York
Dates 1985/86
Project Team *Peter K. Toh,* Edna Guilor, John Patey, Marc Spector, John Seifert, Vincent Franchi

Project Gilison Industries
Location Hicksville, New York
Date 1984
Project Team *Michael Harris Spector,* Dominic Cardone

Project C.W. Post Dormitory
Location Greenvale, New York
Dates 1985/87
Project Team *Peter K. Toh,* Scott Woolsey, William Scherer, Kenneth Wattenberg, Joseph Reilly, Marc Spector, George Kucheck, Vincent Franchi, Khalid Mohammed

Project Hoboken Center
Location Hoboken, New Jersey
Dates 1984/86
Project Team *Peter K. Toh,* Ralph Ottaiano, Edward Butt, Michael McNerney

Project Reliance Center of Long Island
Location Huntington, New York
Dates 1985/86
Project Team *Michael J. Mannetta,* William Medlow, Mike McNerney, Joseph Randazzo, Jeff Friedman

Project Manhasset/Lakeville Firehouse
Location Thomaston, New York
Dates 1984/86
Project Team *Peter K. Toh,* George Kuchek, Michael McNerney, Scott Woolsey, Ianthe Carpen, Donald Oster, Gregory Campofranco, Maria Anza, John Kraft

Project Silver Springs Center
Location Silver Springs, Maryland
Dates 1985/87
Project Team *Michael Harris Spector,* John Giaccio, Peter Toh

Project Metropolis Center
Location New York, New York
Dates 1985/87
Project Team *Michael Harris Spector, Michael J. Mannetta,* Michael Mannetta, Dominic Cardone, Peter Toh, Michael McNerney, Gary Lawrance, Ralph Ottaiano

Project Ronald McDonald House
Location New York, New York
Dates 1985/87
Project Team *Michael Harris Spector, Michael J. Mannetta,* Dominic Cardone, Charles Golub

Project Fleet Bank
Location Melville, New York
Dates 1985/87
Project Team *Michael J. Mannetta,* Joseph Randazzo, Paul Llopis, William Medlow, Stanley Stevens

Project Country Glen Center
Location Carle Place, New York
Dates 1985/87
Project Team *Peter K. Toh, Michael J. Mannetta,* John Gregorio, Gerard Torchio, Thomas Bitnar, Michael McNerney, Joseph Randazzo

Project The Century
Location Great Neck, New York
Dates 1985/87
Project Team *Michael Harris Spector, Peter K. Toh,* Edward Butt, Gerard Torchio, Donald Oster

Project North Sea Insurance Company
Location Valley Stream, New York
Dates 1986/88
Project Team *Michael Harris Spector, Michael J. Mannetta,* Frank Messano, George Kuchek, Gregory Campofranco, Maria Anza, Joseph Reilly, Kin Yan Yan, Charles D'Alessio

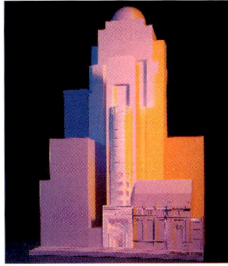

Project Ivy Tower
Location New York, New York
Dates 1985/87
Project Team *Peter K. Toh,* Dominic Cardone, John Seifert, Gary Lawrance, Roger Diller

Project Minolta Headquarters
Location Huntington, New York
Dates 1986/88
Project Team *Michael J. Mannetta,* Frank Messano

Project Atlantic City Hotel
Location Atlantic City, New Jersey
Dates 1985/87
Project Team *Peter K. Toh,* William Medlow, Paul Llopis, Joseph Randazzo

Project General Accident Insurance
Location Melville, New York
Dates 1986/89
Project Team *Michael J. Mannetta,* Frank Mrakovcic, Joe Randazzo, Robert Verbanac, John Kraft, Stanley Stevens, John Machovec, Vincent Franchi, David Rozzi

Project Corporate Center
Location Hunt Valley, New York
Date 1985
Project Team *Peter K. Toh,* Ralph Ottaiano, William Davis, Roger Diller

Project River Run Residential Community
Location Ocean City, Maryland
Dates 1986/88
Project Team *Michael J. Mannetta,* William Medlow, William Davis

Project SA Executive Offices
Location Garden City, New York
Date 1985
Project Team *Michael J. Mannetta,* William Medlow, John Seifert

Project Key Bank
Location Islandia, New York
Dates 1986/89
Project Team *Michael J. Mannetta,* John Gregorio, Greg Basmajian, Vincent Franchi

Project Tenney Mountain Ski Village
Location Plymouth, New Hampshire
Dates 1986/88
Project Team *Michael J. Mannetta, Thomas Bitnar,* Ralph Ottaiano, William Davis, Vincent Franchi, Greg Basmajian

Project Sabena Airlines
Location Manhasset, New York
Date 1986
Project Team *Peter K. Toh,* Pamela Wright Knakal, Gregory Campofranco, Terry Geller, Ianthe Carpen, George Kuchek, Patricia Schachter, Roger Diller, John Seifert

Project Princeton Nurseries
Location Princeton, New Jersey
Date 1986
Project Team *Michael J. Mannetta,* Thomas Bitnar, Michael McNerney, Ralph Ottaiano

Project Guttman Institute
Location New York, New York
Date 1986
Project Team *Peter K. Toh,* Gregory Campofranco, Renee Reichert, Pamela Wright Knakal

Project Maimonides Medical Arts
Location Brooklyn, New York
Dates 1986/90
Project Team *Peter K. Toh,* Tom Moran, Jeff Friedman, Scott Hayden, Thomas Bitnar, Sean Cuddahy, Dominic Cardone, Robert Verbanac

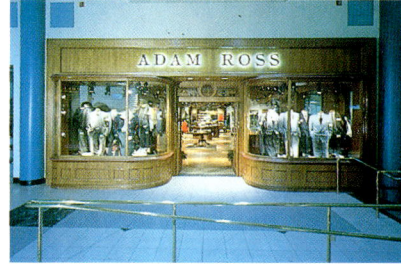

Project Adam Ross
Location Cleveland, Ohio
Date 1987
Project Team *Michael J. Mannetta,* Gregory Campofranco, Kathi Burns

Project Minskoff Residential Condominiums
Location White Plains, New York
Dates 1986/88
Project Team *Peter K. Toh,* Arthur Gentile, Frank Mrakovcic, Chip Calcagni, Thomas Bitnar

Project Long Beach Condominiums
Location Long Beach, New York
Date 1987
Project Team *Peter K. Toh,* Roger Diller, Kathi Burns, Gary Lawrance

Project Carrefour Department Store
Location Holtsville, New York
Date 1986
Project Team *Peter K. Toh,* Frank Messano, Scott Spector, Kathi Burns, Robert Verbanac, Frank Adamowicz

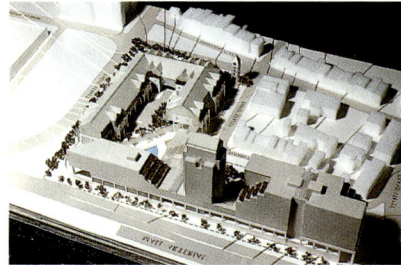

Project Albany Center
Location Albany, New York
Dates 1987/89
Project Team *Peter K. Toh,* Dominic Cardone, Kathi Burns

Project Union Headquarters
Location New York, New York
Dates 1986/88
Project Team *Michael Harris Spector, Michael J. Mannetta,* Peter Toh, Thomas Bitnar

Project Evans Financial Center
Location Smithtown, New York
Dates 1987/89
Project Team *Michael J. Mannetta,* Frank Messano, Greg Basmajian, Joseph Randazzo, John Machovec, Christine Friello

Project Niko Hotel
Location Garden City, New York
Dates 1986/88
Project Team *Peter K. Toh,* William Medlow, Thomas Bitnar

Project Grumman Center
Location Suffolk County, New York
Dates 1987/88
Project Team *Peter K. Toh,* William Medlow, Roger Diller, Paul Llopis

Project Hewlett-Woodmere Schools
Location Hewlett, New York
Dates 1987/90
Project Team *Paul Anderson*, Frank Messano, Marc Spector, Paul Llopis, Ben Videna, Jeanette Sabino, Scott Hayden, Louis Reyes

Project Shelter Rock Collection
Location Manhasset, New York
Dates 1988/90
Project Team *Peter K. Toh*, Joseph Randazzo, Edward Butt, Kathi Burns, Stanley Stevens, Gregory Basmajian, Scott Hayden, Joan Liebman

Project 111 Jericho Turnpike
Location Syosset, New York
Date 1988
Project Team *Michael Harris Spector*, Frank Messano, Paul Llopis, Robert Verbanac, David Rozzi

Project Cerrone/Anton
Location East Meadow, New York
Date 1989
Project Team *Michael J. Mannetta*, Dominic Cardone, Paul Anderson, Marc Spector, Robert Verbanac

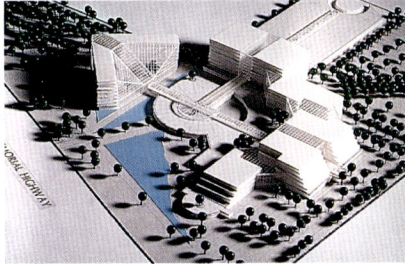

Project Evans International Center
Location Bohemia, New York
Dates 1988/91
Project Team *Michael J. Mannetta*, Frank Messano, Arthur Johnson, John Machovec, Christine Friello

Project Computer Associates
Location Islandia, New York
Dates 1989/1991
Project Team *Peter K. Toh*, Frank Mrakovcic, Arthur Johnson, George Kuchek, John Machovec, Thomas Moran, Paul Llopis, Scott Spector, Scott Hayden, Vincent Franchi, Rick DiFilippi

Project Southgate Corporate Campus
Location Stony Brook, New York
Date 1988
Project Team *Michael J. Mannetta*, Frank Adamowicz, Nick Caivano

Project Olsten Corporation
Location Westbury, New York
Dates 1989/91
Project Team *Michael Harris Spector, Peter Toh*, Arthur Gentile, Ianthe Carpen, Frank Messano,, Marc Spector, John Machovec, Vincent Franchi, Joan Liebman, Kin Yan Yan, Robert Verbanac

Project General Accident Insurance Interiors
Location Melville, New York
Dates 1988/90
Project Team *Michael J. Mannetta*, Frank Mrakovcic, Joseph Randazzo, Kin Yan Yan,, Robert Verbanac, John Machovec, Stanley Stevens, David Rozzi, Vincent Franchi

Project Woodbury Jewish Center
Location Woodbury, New York
Date 1989
Project Team *Michael J. Mannetta*, Joseph Randazzo, Scott Spector, Scott Hayden, Marc Spector, Paul Anderson

Project Zurich American International
Location Huntington, New York
Dates 1988/90
Project Team *Peter K. Toh*, Greg Campofranco, Pamela Wright Knakal, John Seifert

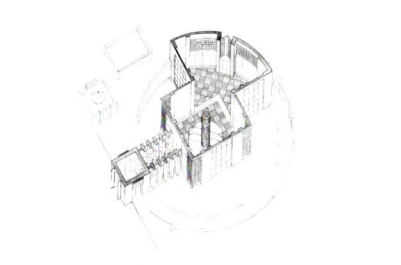

Project Temple Judea Holocaust Resource Center
Location Manhasset, New York
Dates 1992/94
Project Team *Marc B. Spector*, Tom Moran, Scott Hayden, Paul Anderson

Project IBM Marketing Group
Location Jericho, New York
Date 1990
Project Team *Michael J. Mannetta,* Joseph Randazzo, Ralph Ottaiano, Paul Anderson, Vincent Franchi, David Rozzi, Paul Llopis

Project BMW
Location New York, New York
Dates 1991/93
Project Team *Michael J. Mannetta,* Frank Mrakovcic, George Kuchek, Vincent Franchi, Arthur Johnson, Paul Anderson, Scott Hayden, Paul Heretakis

Project Prague Center
Location Prague, Czech Republic
Dates 1990/92
Project Team *Michael Harris Spector, Peter Toh,* Thomas Bitnar, Robert Verbanac, Vincent Affenita

Project Sony Western Regional Operations
Location San Jose, California
Dates 1991/93
Project Team *Michael J. Mannetta, Peter K. Toh,* Thomas Moran, Joseph Randazzo, Arthur Johnson, Ben Videna, John Machovec, Jeanette Sabino, Paul Llopis, Marc Spector

Project Baron Hotel
Location Brussels, Belgium
Dates 1990/92
Project Team *Peter K. Toh,* Charles Croigny, Thomas Bitnar, Paul Llopis, Robert Verbanac

Project Nove Butovice
Location Prague, Czech Republic
Dates 1990/93
Project Team *Michael J. Mannetta,* Thomas Bitnar, Marc Spector, Robert Verbanac, Vincent Affenita

Project Martini Center
Location Brussels, Belgium
Dates 1990/93
Project Team *Peter K. Toh,* Charles Croigny, Thomas Bitnar

Project Olympus America
Location Huntington, New York
Dates 1991/92
Project Team *Michael J. Mannetta, Peter K. Toh,* Scott Spector, Arthur Johnson, Vincent Franchi, Tara Valone, Marc Spector, Scott Hayden, John Machovec, Vincent Franchi, Paul Llopis, Ben Videna

Project Cablevision Executive Center
Location Woodbury, New York
Dates 1990/91
Project Team *Michael J. Mannetta,* Marc Spector, Tom Moran, Ed Friedman, Paul Anderson, Robert Verbanac

Project Federal Building & U.S. Courthouse
Location Islip, New York
Dates 1993/98
Project Team *Richard Meier & Partners,* Michael Harris Spector, Dominic Cardone, George Kuchek, Robert Verbanac, Hayden, John Machovec, Tara Valone, Johnathan Reo, Thomas Fraehmke, Irene Yu, Milan Hospodka, Marcelo Kohan

Project Chase Manhattan Bank
Location New York, New York
Dates 1991/92
Project Team *Scott E. Spector, Peter K. Toh,* Thomas Moran, Ben Videna, Jeanette Sabino, Tara Valone, Robert Verbanac, Vincent Franchi

Project Jiu Hai Plaza
Location Shanghai, China
Dates 1993/97
Project Team *Michael J. Mannetta,* Michael Harris Spector, James Jao, Paul Anderson, George Kuchek, John Machovec, Albert Han, Ci Hang Ping, Lu Zheng Zhong, Jeanette Sabino, Tara Valone, Robert Verbanac, Marc Spector, Paul Anderson, Vincent Affenita

Project Gardens at Great Neck
Location Great Neck, New York
Dates 1993/94
Project Team *Michael J. Mannetta*, Joseph Randazzo, Vincent Franchi, Ben Videna, Paul Anderson

Project Joe Bar Coffee Bar
Location New York, New York
Date 1993
Project Team *Marc B. Spector*, Paul Anderson

Project Snapple Beverage Headquarters
Location East Meadow, New York
Dates 1993/94
Project Team *Marc B. Spector*, Scott Spector, Scott Hayden, Tara Valone, Ben Videna, Arthur Johnson, George Kuchek

Project Samsung Corporate Headquarters
Location Ridgefield Park, New Jersey
Dates 1993/94
Project Team *Peter K. Toh*, Frank Messano, Scott Hayden, Paul Anderson, Robert Verbanac

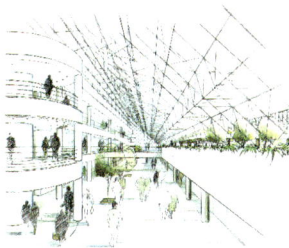

Project Mutual of New York
Location Melville, New York
Dates 1993/94
Project Team *Peter K. Toh*, Joseph Randazzo, Paul Anderson, Vincent Affenita, John Machovec

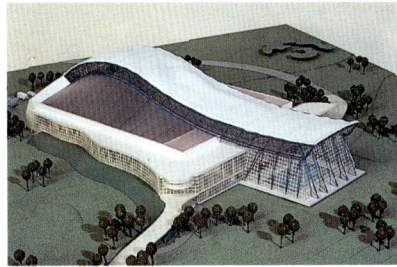

Project 1998 Goodwill Games Aquatic Ctr.
Location East Meadow, New York
Dates 1993/96
Project Team *Michael Harris Spector, Eggers Group*, Thomas Moran, Michael Mannetta

Project Dalian Fashion City Complex
Location Dalian, China
Dates 1993/97
Project Team *Michael J. Mannetta, Paul Anderson,* Michael Harris Spector, James Jao, Paul Anderson, Vincent Affenita, Jeanette Sabino, Scott Hayden

Project Meadowlands Planned Unit Development
Location Bergen County, New Jersey
Dates 1992/97
Project Team *Lawrence Braverman*, Michael Harris Spector, Leo Kornblath, Frank Messano, Dominic Cardone

Project Zhong Hang Plaza
Location Shenzhen, China
Dates 1993/97
Project Team *Michael J. Mannetta*, Michael Harris Spector, James Jao, Paul Anderson, Vincent Affenita, Tara Valone, Robert Verbanac, Vincent Franchi, Jeanette Sabino

Project San Kei Commercial City
Location Shenyang, China
Dates 1993/97
Project Team *Peter K. Toh,* Michael Harris Spector, James Jao, Jeanette Sabino, Scott Hayden

Awards

The following is a list of the significant design awards and honors earned by the Spector Group.

Project	Award	Presented By	Year
Sony Western Regional Operations Center	Award of Merit	Pacific Coast Builders Conference	1994
Hewlett Elementary School, New York	Exhibition of School Architecture	National School Boards Association in cooperation with the American Institute of Architects	1993
Computer Associates, New York Grumman Data Systems, New York Roslyn Highlands Firehouse, New York	Juried Exhibition at International Design Center, New York	Rhode Island School of Design	1992
General Accident Insurance Company, New York	Award of Excellence	Society of American Registered Architects	1992
Woodbury Jewish Center, New York	Excellence In Masonry	Masonry Institute of New York	1992
Long Island Savings Bank Executive Headquarters, New York	Award of Excellence	American Institute of Architects	1991
The Century Condominiums, New York	Merit Award	*Builder* Magazine, Builders' Choice Awards	1991
Grumman Data Systems Headquarters, New York	Award of Excellence	Society of American Registered Architects	1990
Key Bank, New York	Award of Excellence	Society of American Registered Architects	1990
Roslyn Highlands Firehouse, New York	Award of Excellence	Society of American Registered Architects	1990
Country Glen Retail Center, New York	Silver	American Institute of Architects	1988
Manhasset Lakeville Firehouse, New York	Excellence in Masonry	Masonry Institute of New York	1988
Spector Report Newsletter	National First Place	Society for Marketing Professional Services	1988
Merck & Co. Headquarters, New Jersey	Gold	American Institute of Architects	1987
Merrill Lynch Executive Group, New Jersey	First Place	BUILDER Magazine, Builders' Choice Awards	1986
Merrill Lynch Executive Group, New Jersey	Gold	American Institute of Architects	1986
NYNEX Headquarters, New York	Gold	American Institute of Architects	1986
Roslyn Highlands Firehouse, New York	Excellence in Masonry	Masonry Institute of New York	1986
Roslyn Highlands Firehouse, New York	Gold	American Institute of Architects	1986
New York Hilton Renovation, New York	Silver	American Institute of Architects	1986
Grumman Data Systems Headquarters, New York	Silver	American Institute of Architects	1985
European American Bank Headquarters, New York	Silver	American Institute of Architects	1985
Merrill Lynch Executive Center, New Jersey	Governors Good Neighbor Award	New Jersey Business & Industry Association	1985
Hilton Hotel at Somerset Park, New Jersey	Governors Good Neighbor Award	New Jersey Business & Industry Association	1984

Project	Award	Presented By	Year
Manufacturers Hanover Trust, New York	Silver	American Institute of Architects	1984
Spector Group Studios/Offices, New York	Silver	American Institute of Architects	1984
Spector Group Studios/Offices, Interiors	Gold	American Institute of Architects	1984
European American Bank Headquarters, New York	Golden Circle Award	Long Island Forum Association	1984
Stone Oaks Condominiums, New York	Design, Energy, & Construction Excellence	Westchester Builders Institute	1984
European American Bank Headquarters, New York	Award of Merit	Concrete Industry Board of America	1983
IBM Information Systems, New York	Gold	American Institute of Architects	1983
IBM Information Systems, Interiors	Gold	American Institute of Architects	1983
IBM Global Communications, New York	Gold	American Institute of Architects	1983
IBM Global Communications, Interiors	Gold	American Institute of Architects	1983
IBM Information Systems, New York	Certificate of Achievement & Recognition	Builder's Institute of Westchester and Putnam Counties	1982
Avant Garde Optics, New York	Gold	American Institute of Architects	1982
Cushman & Wakefield Corporate Headquarters, New York	Gold	American Institute of Architects	1982
Bikoff Building, New York	First Prize	Borough of Queens Chamber of Commerce	1979
Allstate Insurance Headquarters, New York	Award of Merit	Concrete Industry Board of America	1978
SoMar Dental Studios Offices, New York	First Prize	Borough of Queens Chamber of Commerce	1977
Spector Group Studios, New York	Silver	American Institute of Architects	1976
Eastern Savings Bank, New York	Silver	American Institute of Architects	1975
North Hills Corporate Center, New York	Silver	American Institute of Architects	1975
Great Neck Library & Youth Facility	Silver	American Institute of Architects	1974
Extebank, New York	Silver	American Institute of Architects	1974
Spector Residence, New York	Silver	American Institute of Architects	1973
Great Neck Shopping Tower, New York	Silver	American Institute of Architects	1973
Crossways Office Complex, New York	Silver	American Institute of Architects	1973
Hempstead Office Plaza, New York	Silver	American Institute of Architects	1972
Expressway Office Center, New York	Silver	American Institute of Architects	1971

Michael Harris Spector

Photographers   *Vincent Affenita:* Woodbury Jewish Center

Gil Amiaga: IBM Jericho Plaza, Extebank

Andrew Appell: Dime Savings Bank

Andrew Batson: Metropolis Center

Mert Carpenter: Sony Western Regional Operations Center

Peter K. Cowan: 666 Old Country Road

George Erml: Grumman Data Systems, Horizon One, IBM Research Group,
Ivy Tower, Long Island University, Maimonides, Medical Center,
Merck & Company, Inc., Merrill Lynch Executive Group, Merrill Lynch
Operations Center, NYNEX Headquarters, River Run Community

Jeff Goldberg/Esto: General Accident Insurance Company

Andrew Gordon: Computer Associates International World Headquarters

Andrew Kramer: Century Condominiums, Chase Manhattan Bank,
Country Glen Center, 40 Cuttermill Road, 80 Cuttermill Road,
Grumman Data Systems, Long Island Savings Bank, United States
Postal Service

Thomas Leighton: Fleet Bank Corporate Headquarters,
Key Bank Headquarters

Marco Lorenzetti/Hendrich-Blessing: Computer Associates Interiors

Gregory Murphy: Merrill Lynch Executive Group, European American
Bank Plaza

Peter Roth: Great Neck Estates Apartments

Mark Ross: New York Hilton Hotel

Mark Samu: Hewlett-Woodmere School District, Woodbury Jewish Center

Carl G. Saporiti: Roslyn Highlands Firehouse

Guy Sussman: Allstate Insurance Center

Paul Warchol: Avant Garde Optics

Nick Wheeler: Spector Group Studios

Roy Wright: BMW Showroom and Service Pavilion, Cablevision Corporate
Headquarters, Chase Manhattan Bank, Ronald McDonald House